I1 170

D1380935

L2

COLUMBANUS COMMUNITY LIBRARY
683 ANTRIM ROAD

CANCELLED 11 MAR 2013

Irish School of Ecumenics
D 0019978

# Law, love and language

COLUMBANUS COMMUNITY LIBRARY
683 ANTRIM ROAD

# Law, love and language

Herbert McCabe OP

Sheed and Ward · London and Sydney

First published 1968
Sheed and Ward Ltd, 33 Maiden Lane, London WC2, and
Sheed and Ward Pty Ltd, 95 York Street, Sydney
© Herbert McCabe 1968

Imprimi potest: Ian Hislop OP, Provincial
Nihil obstat: Lionel Swain, STL, LSS, Censor
Imprimatur: + Patrick Casey, Vicar General
Westminster, 1 June 1968

Standard book number 7220 0542 3
This book is set in 12/14 pt Monotype Plantin
Made and printed in Great Britain by
William Clowes and Sons Ltd, London and Beccles

# Contents

To John and Harden

and

most of them in McDaid's

# Preface

This book has grown out of the Chaplaincy Open Lectures which I was invited to deliver at the University of Kent in Canterbury during the Lent Term of 1968 and I would like to begin by thanking the Vice-Chancellor and the Revd Frank Telfer who with the other chaplains organised the series. I must also thank Professor James Cameron for his hospitality, encouragement and helpful criticism during my visits. I single him out from the many others who made my stay so enjoyable because he let me have the use of his flat. Most of all I want to thank the many students who sat around in that flat until a late hour and explained the various mistakes I had made. I hope they will find this revised and expanded version an improvement.

I have to thank Mr Jonathan Power and the

other signatories of the *Haslemere Declaration* for permission to reproduce an extract from it as an appendix, and similarly to thank the editor of *New Blackfriars* for permission to reprint Appendix 2. Quotations from scripture, where no other reference is given, are taken from the Jerusalem Bible.

Herbert McCabe OP
Blackfriars, Oxford
Easter 1968

# 1
# Ethics as love

In these essays I want to take a quick look at three starting-points from which we might think about ethics, three different ways of throwing light on what ethics is all about. None of them is a complete account of ethics and I think at least the first two are fairly seriously inadequate; nevertheless they may each be of some help. The three points of departure are roughly: ethics is a matter of loving, ethics is a matter of obeying the law, and ethics is a matter of talking to people. These do not represent three mutually exclusive views; whichever one you take, you will certainly claim that it can accommodate all that is good in the others, but it makes a difference which one is your fundamental model. It will make a certain practical difference to the moral judgements you make, but it will make a much more important practical difference to the moral judgements you do not make. I mean that if you hold an inadequate theory of ethics you are liable to ignore some important moral questions. It is this that makes the discussion important.

In this first chapter I am going to look at the proposition 'all you need is love' to see whether it will do as a basic model for ethics. Next I want to look at a version of the idea of moral law or natural law—the idea that ethics is fundamentally a matter of recognising and acknowledging the basic laws of human nature. In both cases I shall try to give reasons why I think these models are not quite good enough. In the third chapter I shall try to develop the idea that ethics has to do with communication, with the fact that human animals make use of conventional signs and symbols. Finally I shall try to discover what difference is made by the fact that men communicate not merely in a human language but in the language of God, that we share in the word of God.

There is a fairly widespread view, at least in western Europe and America, that when we ask about morals we are asking whether a man is loving or not. If an action is an act of love then it is good, if not then it is bad or at least merely tolerable. It is important to the version of this view that we shall be examining that we are not in the end concerned with the physical details of the activity, how it looks from outside, but with whether or not it was done out of love. What looks exactly the same piece of behaviour may in one case be done from love and in another not; our moral judgement is solely concerned with determining this matter. Thus the same sexual behaviour—and the moralists of this school are particularly interested in sexual behaviour—may be in one case an act of genuine love and in another a matter of selfishness or domination. They are particularly insistent that the mere legal form of marriage cannot transform a piece of bad sexual behaviour into a good one, nor does the absence of marriage necessarily make a piece of otherwise good behaviour bad. It is ridiculous, they would say, to make it a *principle* that sexual relations outside marriage are bad while within marriage they are good. You may, and probably will conclude that this is usually the case, but the determining principle is not the presence or absence of marriage but of love.

Part of the attractiveness of this position is that it seems to avoid what has been called the 'naturalistic fallacy', the idea that values can be derived from facts, or that we can tell from a mere description of a state of affairs that it ought or ought not to be brought about. Few doctrines are more firmly established in the orthodoxy of the present time than the belief that the world of objective facts is one thing and the world of subjective values is quite another. Two men whose views about what *ought* to be the case are wholly different can, it is said, if they are sufficiently cool and unemotional, come to exactly the same conclusions about what actually *is* the case. Conversely, they may be in complete agreement about all the facts and yet come to quite different moral conclusions. It is therefore a mistake to suppose that any state of affairs or piece of behaviour could be intrinsically good or bad, simply in virtue of what it is. I shall have a little more to say about this doctrine later on, for it will be clear that any idea that moral law can be derived from a consideration of the nature of man must be open to the accusation that it involves the naturalistic fallacy. For the moment it is sufficient to notice that the view that 'all you need is love' with its insistence that no moral character attaches to any piece of external behaviour as such, seems to avoid any such accusation.

The view is particularly common amongst christian theologians in our time and it is generally thought to have something especially christian about it; and with good reason. There is not only a great deal of quotable stuff in the New Testament about the primacy of love, but the opposition between Jesus and the scribes and pharisees, which is a major theme of the gospels, turns upon the question of law and love. They are legalists, insisting on the minute observance of the law; he shows how heartless this law can be and appeals against it to human love and concern for others. In one sense this opposition to legalism is a central and permanent part of the christian gospel; there is, however, another sense in which such opposition involves a criticism of christianity. The christian church is always under the temptation to develop its own legalism, to lay down its own rules, to codify moral behaviour for men. Members of the church in every age are called to the prophetic task of bringing christianity once more into line with the gospel, breaking through christian legalism to a more truly christian freedom. The church is constantly liable to betray her mission and is in constant need of reformation.

A defender of natural law is, however, entitled to argue, as for example Aquinas argues, that Jesus on no occasion sets aside the *moral* law in favour of love.[1] A less cursory examination of

[1] 'Lex nova non evacuat observantiam veteris legis nisi quantum ad caeremonialia.' *Summa Theologica* I–II 107. 2. ad I. cf 108. 2. c.

the texts shows that what he is setting aside are the customs and ritual practices of Israel. 'The sabbath is made for man and not man for the sabbath.' (Mk 2:27) Indeed he explicitly opposes such traditional rules to the *commandment* of God: 'Why do you transgress the commandment of God for the sake of your tradition?' (Mt 15:3) Jesus is not here recommending us to set aside the law of God for the sake of love; he is recommending that we uphold it against the traditions of men. The command he refers to is undoubtedly the command to love God and one's neighbour on which 'depends all the law and the prophets' (Mt 22:40), and so we may say that he upholds the demands of love as against human traditions; but this is a very different thing from opposing love to moral law. The advocates of the doctrine that 'all you need is love' have too hastily assumed that the provisional character that the New Testament writers attribute to religious customs and observances should also attach to the moral law itself. I think it must be admitted that the New Testament provides no explicit grounds for the idea that the moral law may be provisional—any more than it provides such grounds for, say, the episcopacy or the sacramental character of marriage.

Amongst many christians, however, the doctrine of the primacy of love is seen as a reaction against legalism, and legalism is taken to include any notion of an absolute moral law. It is well to be clear, at this point, about the meaning of 'absolute' in this context. It means simply 'independent'. If, for example, a man holds that there is an absolute prohibition on telling lies he means that if a man's behaviour could correctly be described by saying 'he is telling a lie' then his behaviour is prohibited, quite independently of whatever other descriptions might be given of his action. Take the case of the officer of the Saigon regime who returned home recently to find that his wife and child had been killed, presumably by a member of the National Liberation Front. Various descriptions could be given of the behaviour of the man who killed the officer's child. He was perhaps punishing the officer for atrocities he had committed in the past, he was discouraging others from supporting the corrupt policies of the Saigon government, he was helping to liberate the Vietnamese people, he was killing this child, he was firing his gun in this direction . . . and so on. Evidently there are an indefinite number of such descriptions. Now if you hold, for example, that the deliberate killing of children is absolutely wrong, then you hold that no matter what else occurs in the list, so long as it contains the description 'he was killing this child' then the action was wrong and should not have been done.

It is quite important to notice that being absolutely wrong is not the same as being very very wrong. A man might hold that lying is absolutely wrong while at the same time regarding it as often a rather trivial offence. All that 'absolutely' says is that whatever makes it wrong is independent of circumstances. A relativist who does not accept any absolute moral laws may still have moral convictions that are just as intense as those of the absolutist.

The absolutist, then, would say that if a piece of behaviour is defective in some particular respect (if it comes under an absolute prohibition) then whatever else may be good about it is irrelevant. However splendid my television set may be, it is useless if the current is switched off. Other moralists would say that you have to consider the whole pattern of possible descriptions of an action; no single element in it can by itself and independently make the action bad, just as no single brushstroke can make a painting ugly; it depends on what surrounds it. I shall be arguing later that this latter view runs up against two difficulties; one concerns the size of the painting—when to put a frame round it and say 'here we have the total picture'; the other concerns learning the meaning of words such as 'beautiful' and 'ugly'; but for the moment let us look at some of the difficulties that an absolutist runs into.

It is not difficult to find, or at least to imagine, the human tragedies which might result from the strict application of absolute moral principles. Consider, for example, the classical example of therapeutic abortion. It seems, on the face of it, harmless enough to maintain as an absolute principle that the lives of at least the people who are not actively trying to harm you are sacred—that an innocent person has a right to his life. It also seems unreasonable to say that a child only becomes human when he leaves the womb. You might not be sure how far to go here; you might be vague about just when you would start calling him human, but I suppose everyone would agree that for some time the pregnant woman has in her womb a human person. Hence it seems harmless enough to maintain that this human person, like anyone else, has a right to life.

But then consider the extraordinary situation that sometimes used to arise, when medicine was in a less advanced stage, when owing to various complications both mother and child were obviously on the way to dying. In this situation you had just two courses open to you: you either killed the child, in which case there was a good chance of saving the life of the mother, or else you didn't kill the child, in which case not only did the mother die, but the child died as well. The absolutist would seem to be committed to the latter course because he would never think it right in any circumstances to kill an innocent person. And so you get the paradoxical state of affairs that the absolutist seems, precisely because of his respect for human life, to have brought about two deaths, whereas the relativist, who is prepared to perform the abortion, at least saves the life of the mother.

The paradox is not real, however. It is not the absolutist's respect for life that has led him to accept the deaths; it is the fact that this respect is expressed in an absolute prohibition. The relativist could well claim to have more respect for human life. 'But my respect,' he might say, 'isn't expressed in fine intransigent moral gestures, but in actually saving lives.' We may notice here what is almost a clash of temperament between the man who stands by a principle come what may, and the man who is prepared to compromise on principles for the sake of improving things a little. This conflict between revolutionary and reformer is one that will occupy us from time to time in these pages.

I may say here in passing that I think the absolutist need not be overthrown by a case such as this. He may argue that ethics is not supposed to be an absolutely comprehensive coherent theory, such as should be tested by seeing how it fares in crucial marginal cases; it is, on the contrary, intended to be a practical skill in the affairs of every day. Cases such as the one we have outlined, after all, hardly ever come up, and in the meantime in the ordinary business of life where heroism and difficult choices may quite frequently be required, which attitude is likely to produce the more admirable person, that of the absolutist or that of the relativist? The answer is not a foregone conclusion but the question is a genuine one. I think that though the absolutist formulates his position in terms of single decisions—'this is something that I simply must never do'—his position is at its most plausible when we see it not as determining particular decisions but as determining a whole style of life.

I have raised the hoary question of therapeutic abortion not for its own sake but merely to illustrate the kind of difficulty, even absurdity, that you might get into by the strict application of rules. In the case of any rule of action you can almost always imagine a situation in which the slavish following of the rule will defeat the purpose for which the rule was made. The people who advocate love as a basis for ethics take a different view of the place of rules in moral life. For them laws and rules are guidelines to the demands of love. Although any human situation is unique, there is a sufficient similarity between some situations for us to draw up broad generalisations about the appropriate loving behaviour: moral laws are nothing but such rules of thumb. This does not mean that moral laws are unimportant; on the contrary, without them we should have great difficulty in coming to moral decisions at all. Moral laws represent the accumulated wisdom of the ages: they tell us what, in general, men have found it best to do in certain situations, but they leave us in the end to make our own judgements.

Moral laws, according to this view, are something like the 'rules' of an art. We can be taught how to paint or to carve, we can learn the laws of perspective and so on, but the great works of art are not necessarily produced by an exact obedience to these rules. A man will hardly ever be a great artist unless he has learned the traditional rules, but his greatness will often show itself in knowing just when to ignore them or go beyond them. Certainly the *test* of a great work of art is not whether it is constructed according to the rules. We can indeed frequently say of a bad work of art that the man just doesn't know how to draw. . . . We can, in fact, often *condemn* something and give as our reason that it breaks the rules; but when we praise something it is not because it obeys the rules, even when it does; moreover, sometimes the very breaking of the rules may contribute to its success. On the other hand we sometimes find ourselves speaking of a painting as competent (in accordance with the rules) but lifeless and uninteresting.

Now according to the view I am at present considering, moral judgements are very similar to this. We have to go through a moral apprenticeship in which we learn to follow the moral laws that have been handed down to us, and this is a necessary stage if we are ever to learn to be free, to make our own judgements. Nevertheless in the crucial case, in the great choices in which we make or unmake our lives, we may find that the truly loving act demands that we ignore or go beyond the rules. It is true that there are a great many blameworthy actions, and it is true that for nearly all of these we can say quite simply why they are wrong, we can point to the rule they have broken —just as there are a great many bad drawings and we can point to the rule that has been broken in their case too. But the important praiseworthy act is not great because it keeps the rules, and it may be great just because it involves the courage to break them. The legalist's mistake, in this view, is to make an idol of his laws, an idol that occasionally demands human sacrifice.

This view of morals is, I think, a fairly familiar one and it is one I personally find extremely attractive, but it eventually runs into difficulties, and these we ought now to consider. The first difficulties concern the meaning of the word 'love'. It is not, in the first place, absolutely clear what relationship love is supposed to have to behaviour. Let us consider first an extreme view: love is something wholly different from behaviour, so that the question of whether a man is loving or not is an entirely different question from whether he behaves in this or that way. Any attempt to decide whether a man was loving or not by considering his behaviour would then be simply futile. This conclusion might be supposed to commend itself to christians because they are taught that they must not judge other people, and in any case it is notorious that our judgements of others are exceedingly fallible and very vulnerable to our prejudices. However, the view we are considering goes a good deal further than that. The conclusion is not simply that it is undesirable or rash to judge others but that it is quite simply impossible. We can no more decide whether a man is loving or not by looking at his behaviour than we can by tossing a coin. Moreover there is worse to come: not only could we never decide whether another was loving or not, we should have no means of knowing whether we ourselves were loving. Ordinarily I should say that I loved Mary Jane only if I were concerned about her welfare, respected her and so on, and I should know this to be the case because I found myself disposed to act in certain ways when she was around or was in some way affected by my actions. The dispositions and actions involved may be exceedingly complicated—love may express itself in the most surprising ways—but if there is literally nothing that would count as an expression of love, then it is hard to see how I could use the word at all. Theoretically I suppose I might use the word to mean some interior experience which may or may not happen to accompany my external behaviour—rather like a sharp twinge of headache. But then it is hard to see why such an interior experience should be regarded as of fundamental ethical importance. To devote one's life to cultivating this experience need be no more ethically interesting than devoting one's life to getting high on marijuana; moreover if there is really no connection between love and external behaviour it is hard to see how one would set about devoting one's life to its cultivation.

Exponents of the primacy of love do not in fact adopt this extreme position, they merely sometimes slip into talking as though they did. They really want to say that love cannot be defined by describing a piece of loving behaviour and moreover that we cannot describe a piece of behaviour that will always be unloving. Moral laws consist of descriptions of pieces of behaviour which are said to be either compulsory or prohibited, and what is being asserted is that love is never commensurate with moral laws, just as art is never commensurate with 'rules of art'. Love is only loosely related to external behaviour and since laws have to be about such behaviour and since ethics is about love, laws cannot be about what ethics is about.

Come back for a moment to the analogy of the painting. No single detail can make the picture irrevocably ugly; it depends on what surrounds it. The question of whether the painting is ugly or not depends on an overall view of the whole pattern, not on whether it contains certain forbidden patches. Now laws designate certain patches (certain ways of describing an action) as compulsory or prohibited, whereas love has to do with the whole pattern of an action, the act seen in its total situation. The question is not 'could we describe this action in this way (killing a child, for example)?' but 'when we have looked at all the available relevant descriptions, how does the whole pattern look?' An action which in one total situation might seem clearly unloving, might in another be an act of love.

It is undoubtedly true that the relationship of love to behaviour is complex; I mean we cannot describe what it is like for a man to be loving as easily as we can describe what it is like for a man to be walking. These complications arise, I believe, because 'love' is one of those words whose meaning is constantly expanding for us. I mean by this to contrast it with words like 'jam-jar' or 'perhaps'. We discover at a fairly early age how these words are used, it does not require a great deal of intellectual skill, and a mature experienced man of sixty will probably be no better at using them than a boy of six. There are, however, other words, and 'love' is one of them, that are much more complicated in their use. We no doubt begin with some fairly simple range of situations in which we can use the word, a fairly narrow range of behaviour that we would think of as loving. Your mother's love seems practically to consist of being near you, paying attention to you, and giving you what you want. As you grow older you realise that lots of other apparently irrelevant or even apparently hostile acts—like leaving you alone while she cooks your dinner—may be part of a pattern of loving behaviour. A large part of the business of growing up consists in recognising the complex forms that love may take and—this is most important—being open to the possibility of new forms. 'Love' is thus what we might call a growing word, one whose meaning changes and develops, but this does not in the least imply that it is a vague word, one that might mean almost anything. It is just that a word like 'love' will always have uses that are not constricted by such rules for its use as you have managed to formulate at any particular time. We can use the word to try to mean more than we could explain at any time. (That is why it is one of the words we use when we are trying to mean something about God.)

Knowing how to use this word is an essentially historical or autobiographical matter. I mean when you have achieved some skill in the use of the word, you cannot simply hand over your results to someone else; he has to live through the whole business himself, starting with the simplest and crudest understanding. You cannot *start* by having a sophisticated understanding of the matter (as you cannot *start* by having a sophisticated taste in music or literature). If your understanding does not reach down to primitive roots it will not be a live understanding and so it will not be able truly to grow—it may change but it will have no life within it directing it which way to change; it will change mechanically at the mercy of outside forces and fashions. Perhaps we have here moved too far into metaphor.

I mean that there are no short cuts to understanding what love is. If you have been deprived, for example, of the crudest infantile experience of love then you will probably be permanently crippled; at least you will have the greatest difficulty in really grasping the concept in later life. You can pick up the meaning of the word 'jam-jar' any time just by being told the rules, but this is not true of such words as 'love'.

I think there is a useful comparison here between the growth in a man's understanding of a word like 'love' and the large scale historical growth in understanding that Roman catholics, for the last century, have called the 'development of dogma'. Here the same openness, the capacity to produce new and unexpected formulations of faith, is directed by an inner continuity with primitive roots—what is known as the tradition of the gospel. Without the openness to change the church would be static and dead; without the continuity her changes would be arbitrary, directed not by her own immanent life but by the varying fashions of the day.

If our understanding of the word 'love' is in such a constant state of development, we cannot simply tie it down to the range of behaviour which we at present see as loving behaviour. Moreover the situation is further complicated by the fact that we cannot simply *see* the loving behaviour of others as we might see their prowess at football. Just as we cannot see another's argument unless we are responding to it and arguing ourselves, so certain kinds of loving behaviour are only recognisable through our own loving response.

In spite of these complexities I have alleged that 'love' is not a vague word. I think it would be vague if one of the consequences drawn by the advocates of the primacy of love were correct. We cannot be sure beforehand what might turn out to be loving behaviour, but if we can't say of any behaviour at all that it is definitely *not* loving behaviour, then I think the word 'love' would be hopelessly vague. I mean that if a word is to be meaningful there must be at least something that it doesn't mean, however open-ended it may otherwise be.

To go back to our comparison with the tradition of the church. If the teaching of the church is to have any meaning at all there must be at least some things that do not count as the christian gospel. It must be possible for a christian to say 'I don't know how they will be formulating christianity in the twenty-fourth century, but at least I know they won't be arians or nestorians.' Now if, in a parallel way, we are prepared to admit that there must be some kinds of human behaviour that could not count as loving behaviour we are admitting the possibility of absolute prohibitions. By all means let us say that the only thing that is good in all circumstances is love and the only thing that is unequivocally bad is the denial of love, but if our statement is to be meaningful at all we must be able to spell it out by pointing to at least some things that would count as a denial of love. Now a man who says that killing babies is always wrong may not, after all, be a legalist seeking to stifle man's creative inspiration under a load of rules and regulations. He may be simply trying to explain what love means to him—whatever it comes to mean, it can't mean *this*.

Such negative limits to the meaning of love will not, of course, serve as a foundation for ethics, though we are all, I suppose, familiar with attempts to make them serve. The method of the double negative—'being good consists in not doing what you are not allowed to do'—has been a strong favourite with teachers, parents and clergy for many years. But it is one thing to say that prohibitions cannot be the basis of ethics and quite another to deny their validity[1]; without them, as it seems to me, since they are the indispensable minimal rules of meaning for the word 'love', ethics must collapse into complete vagueness. It does not seem to me that the advocates of the primacy of love and of the relative unimportance of law have always faced the pos-

[1] Thus, for example, Aquinas held that conformity to the moral law was a necessary but by no means a sufficient condition for good action. For him the new law consists in the grace of the Holy Spirit. 'Id autem quod est potissimum in lege novi testamenti, et in quo tota virtus eius consistit, est gratia Spiritus Sancti, quae datur per fidem Christi. Et ideo principaliter lex nova est ipsa gratia Spiritus Sancti, quae datur Christi fidelibus.' (I–II 106. I. c.) He held that love is the *forma* of all virtues (I–II 23. 8. c.) by which he meant it was their soul or principle of life. Just as an animal deprived of its life may for a while continue to look like a real animal although it is in fact an altogether different substance (a group of chemicals instead of an organism—Aquinas thought that to use the word 'dog' of a dead dog was to equivocate) so any 'virtue' deprived of love is a mere corpse of a virtue. 'Chastity', let us say, which is not a manifestation of love is merely the corpse of true chastity: it may resemble it outwardly for a while but it will soon rot away and lose even the semblance of the genuine virtue.

sibility that their notion of love may, in this way, become completely vacuous.

If the word 'love' is not to become vague there is at least one other requirement. The meaning of the word may develop in various unexpected and indeed unpredictable ways but after any such development we must subsequently be able to find a continuity of meaning. I think we have an example of non-continuity in the case of the word 'democracy'. This word has probably lost almost all its meaning. It is not that we find new and unexpected forms of democracy—as in Tanzania, for example—which are quite different from the British form, it is just that if you call, say, South Vietnam a democracy, you are plainly doing so out of politeness rather than because you detect some continuity with the meaning of the word in other contexts.

If we are to speak of a genuine growth in our understanding of the word 'love', then however unexpected or even unpredictable a new development may be, it must *subsequently* be seen as in continuity with what has gone before. There is an important difference here between prediction and hindsight. A real development creates a new kind of continuity within which the old is contained as well as transcended. Every creative advance of a living thing restates the whole of its history as a new kind of unity. To revert to our comparison with the development of dogma: it is not incumbent on a Roman catholic to show how the doctrine of papal infallibility could have been accepted or predicted in the third century, but it is incumbent on him to show how this doctrine so transforms our understanding of christianity that from our standpoint in the twentieth century we can now see a continuity. I do not myself think that Roman catholics have been particularly successful in this respect as yet, but they recognise it as a task to be performed.

Now it seems to me that this requirement also is one that is not taken sufficiently seriously by the advocates of the primacy of love. They pass too hastily from the fact that some demands of love are unpredictable to the idea that love escapes the demands of systematic coherence. It is one thing to say that love may in a new situation make demands which could not be anticipated within our system of rules, and quite another to say that love is something separate from such rules. The new and unpredictable act of love belongs to the framework of rules because it changes them. It is one of the tests of a genuine 'exception' to the rules that it has this catastrophic effect—that we do not simply return afterwards to the old formulations as though nothing had happened. In other words even if we cannot fully justify a decision before we make it, we can only claim that it was an act of love if we are prepared to justify it afterwards in terms of a new overall vision. The test of whether a child has broken the rules merely because he is naughty or whether he has really grown out of them is simply whether he has found integration at a new level of maturity, whether he has re-written his autobiography. This latter point perhaps requires some explanation.

A creative advance in love so shifts our moral perspective that we are able to see our whole way of life, and thus ourselves and thus our biography, in a new light. In *1984* George Orwell caricatures a truth. In his society it is found necessary every now and then to re-write all the history books in order to justify shifts in current policy. One version of the past is constantly being discarded in favour of another. I think it is part of Orwell's fundamentally empiricist and liberal approach that he should present this re-writing as intrinsically absurd. For the empiricist there are just the historical facts; to re-write history can only mean mucking about with the facts. Facts are sacred, comment, however, is free; one may draw whatever 'lesson' one likes from the facts, but a mere change in the comment does not involve a re-writing of the history itself. This neat division of facts (which are a matter of truth) from comment (which is a matter of values) is reminiscent of the division made in speaking of the 'naturalistic fallacy' and I believe it to be characteristic of the liberal world-view, which itself has roots in certain economic structures of society. Very roughly the bourgeois industrialised society is one in which men come into relationship, form a community, hence come to agreement and thus to 'truth', only in terms of production. What lies outside this sphere is free, is not a matter of agreement, is 'subjective'. The world of hard facts is the world in which the factories are working, wages are being paid, goods are being distributed; this is the area of necessary agreement in the bourgeois society. Such a society does not require agreement in matters of aesthetics, religion, or 'private morals'; these belong to the sphere of comment and are relegated first to private judgement and then, as their social irrelevance becomes clearer, to the subjective world of 'values'.

As against this liberal empiricist view of history, I should maintain that after a revolution a society *must* re-write its history; it must, that is to say, re-create its identity. I would like to delay on this point a little longer because I think it helps us to understand how the moral life may be neither simply a matter of adhering to a fixed set of rules nor yet abandonment of law in favour of the immediate demands of 'love'.

A revolution is never intelligible in terms of the society it supersedes; but that society must be intelligible in terms of the revolution. Adult life cannot be understood in terms of childhood, but it is part of maturity to understand and accept one's childhood. Consider a society in which there are a certain number of abuses and corruptions. The reformer proposes to remedy these abuses as far as he can. Finding the negroes living in the horrific conditions of the ghetto, he proposes to introduce them to a version of the life of the suburbs. His programme is perfectly intelligible. He does not depart from the accepted values of society, he merely points to the fact that these values are not being realised in certain cases and proposes adjustments so that society will run more smoothly and, in its own terms, more justly. What is wanted, he reckons, is a quantitative change so that more people can share in the same way of life. The reformer will, perhaps, be puzzled by the resistance he meets in carrying out what seems a perfectly rational and desirable programme. Such resistance may be due to the fact, unnoticed by the reformer, that the differential between ghetto and suburb is a necessary part of the structure of the society. Either for economic reasons or, as seems more likely, for much more complex cultural reasons, the suburbs need the ghetto to establish their own identity.

It is then the turn of the revolutionary. He proposes to change not merely this or that detail within society, but the structure, and hence the values of the society itself. The revolutionary does not propose something that in terms of *this* society is better; he wants to change he terms. He wants history to advance not imply further along the established lines, but along new lines. Now such lines extend into the past as well as into the future. I mean that each society interprets its history as leading up to itself, as well as leading forward into the future. Indeed each society *is* its interpretation of its past; just as each person *is* his interpretation of his past. I hope that does not sound too enigmatic. I only mean that if you ask yourself the question 'who am I?' you answer by producing an autobiography. A radical change in society, a revolution, means a change in its interpretation of history, just as a radical change in a person, a conversion let us say, involves a change in the whole of his autobiography. He *now* sees that he was a miserable sinner even though while he was committing the miserable sins he was really rather cheerful about it all.

A creative, revolutionary change, then, even though it is not a mere advance along the old lines of continuity, but a discovery of new lines, does not fully realise itself until it can be seen as in a new kind of continuity with the past. The revolution is not consolidated until it sees itself as the 'natural' fulfilment of the aspirations of the people.

Now I think that 'going beyond the rules' is a kind of revolutionary change. It is not justified if it merely provides a convenient exception but only if it provides a new perspective within which all decisions are revised.

Let us see where we have got to in the argument. For the theory I am criticising, moral laws are simply empirical generalisations; for me they are rules of meaning for the word 'love'. If I am right about this then at least two consequences follow. In the first place the moral laws must exclude certain kinds of behaviour—there must be some things which do not count as love. In the second place although, since the word 'love' is what I have called a growing word, our meaning may sometimes outstrip our semantic rules, there must be at least a 'revolutionary continuity' between what love now means for us and what it used to mean.

If moral laws were merely empirical generalisations of the form 'we have generally found that if Fred loves Charlie he will not beat him senseless with a poker whenever he gets the chance', there would be no cause for surprise if we found occasional exceptions to the rule. It might never have occurred to us before that dropping napalm on children could be an act of love, but it need not surprise us deeply. On my view, on the other hand, a departure from what has hitherto been seen as the law is momentous; it must involve you in a total re-appraisal of yourself and your world. If it does not do so then it is an inauthentic departure; it is, as it were, a mere riot rather than a revolution—not transcending the law but merely failing to keep it. On my view, moreover, the attitude to the law is absolutist until the law is creatively broken. I hope that sounds sufficiently paradoxical. I have said that a revolution is never intelligible in terms of the society that precedes it. So far as that society is concerned, the new way of seeing things that will come in with the revolution is outside and beyond it. A society can allow for certain adjustments and exceptions within its own structure, but it cannot allow for the revolutionary change that will alter its own structures. The two can only be seen as continuous *after* the revolution has occurred. In a parallel way the current form of certain moral laws will always be absolute. We do not say 'it is nearly always wrong to do so and so, though there may be unforeseen cases in which it would be right'. We say simply 'it is always wrong to do so and so'. The unforeseen cases in which it would be right will, if they occur at all, provide their own justification which will mean a re-writing of the whole system of laws. Of course the cases in which we want to say 'it is always wrong to do so and so' will be rather rare but, as I have suggested, without such absolute prohibitions morality collapses into unmeaning.

'The morally good act is not the act prescribed antecedently by some moral law, it is whatever love demands in a particular situation.' I have already suggested some difficulties about this proposition connected with the meaning of the word 'love'; there are perhaps more obvious difficulties connected with the other key word 'situation'. How big is my situation? I mean does it mean the people immediately around me, whom I know, or does it extend to everyone who may be affected by my activities? We may think of the 'situation' in terms of face to face 'personal' relations, but we may also think of it in terms of 'impersonal' social and political relationships. On the whole I think that advocates of 'situation ethics' tend to think mainly in terms of the immediate face to face situation. Their examples of moral problems tend to be taken from the field of family or personal relationships which can fairly plausibly be thought of, at least at first sight, as isolated 'situations' concerning only a few people who know each other. If this is so, then the situationist has two difficulties. Firstly, is he not neglecting what may be the major moral problems of our time, political, social and economic problems? Secondly, is he not arbitrarily supposing that concern for people he knows should take preference over concern for others? Why should my behaviour be governed by my love for these particular people merely because they happen to be within my situation; should I not also consider the people who do not have that privilege? It is likely, however, that we here do an injustice to the situationist. Although his examples happen to be chosen from the family circle, so to speak, he does not restrict the field of morals to matters of immediate encounter. He is prepared to extend the 'situation' to include much wider fields of relationship. In deciding what to do we have to accede to the demands that love makes in the total social and political world in which we find ourselves. This is a much less vulnerable moral position but it is, unfortunately, quite empty. Every moral problem of the slightest interest is a problem about who is to get hurt; the injunction to love everyone concerned does not help us to decide that question. Mr E. M. Forster once remarked 'if I had to choose between betraying my country and betraying my friend, I hope I should have the guts to betray my country'. This is a clear and informative moral position coming down firmly on the side of the personal face to face relationship as against the impersonal social relationship. The opposite message giving preference to the political would be equally clear, but a mere exhortation never to be guilty of betrayal does not help us in any way.

The fact is that any man at any time is in a great number of overlapping situations, the demands of which will frequently conflict. He is a married man with a family, he is also the priest in charge of a parish; he is a shop steward, he is also in the same church as the manager; he is a member of a monastic community, he is also a political activist, and so on. The problem is not so much to discern the demands of 'the' situation as to discern the priorities amongst the different situations. We shall be looking, in the next chapter, at one attempt to solve that problem. The theory of natural law—or at any rate the theory of natural law that I shall be discussing—is an attempt to identify at least the primary situation in which any man must find himself, the situation whose demands must take priority over those of all others; this is the situation of mankind as a whole. According to this view the fundamental and ineluctable fact about my behaviour, and the one that gives rise to absolute moral laws, is that it takes place amongst my fellow men; the first demands made upon me are the demands made by the community of the human race.

# 2 Ethics as law

The term ‘natural law’ covers a wide variety of theories and I have no intention of providing a survey of these or a history of the natural law tradition. Again, views about the content of natural law have ranged from the austerity of the single precept ‘good is to be done and evil to be avoided’, which is not very helpful, to a profusion of quite detailed regulations about the sexual life, which are a positive hindrance. I shall do no more than indicate the areas in which I should expect a natural law to operate. I want to sketch out one possible view which could, I think, reasonably be called a natural law theory; while I do not think it is a good enough account of ethics, I think it throws a good deal of light on the matter.

To be subject to law is to be a member of a community; law is, if you like, the bearing of the community as such on its individual members. There are certain things I do which you might find puzzling if you just thought of me as an isolated individual but which become intelligible once you see me as a member of a group. The law of the United Kingdom is the law I am subject to as a citizen of that country and somewhat similarly the natural law would be the law I am subject to as a member of the community I belong to by nature, the law of mankind. It will, of course, be clear that to make any sense of that remark, you have to stretch the meaning both of 'community' and of 'law' a good deal. In what sense can we speak of mankind as a community, and how can it be said to have a system of laws? It is a curious way of speaking but one that I think is worth persisting in as far as we can. I even think we could speak of sanctions for disobeying the laws of mankind, the penalty of imprisonment—or not being able to do what you want.

Let us begin with the idea of mankind as a community. What is it that makes mankind a unity? There are two kinds of answer to this and it is the intertwining of the two that makes for all the paradoxes. In the first place mankind is a *biological* unity; human beings are interfertile. In order to be human you have to be born of other human beings, you have to be linked by physical genetic relationship with the rest of the human race; mankind, in fact, is an animal species. In the second place mankind is a *linguistic* unity; in order to be human you must, in principle at least, be able to communicate by conventional signs with other human beings. Just as sexual relations and offspring are in principle possible between any man and any woman, so it is in principle possible for any human being to talk any human language. What I mean by 'in principle' here is that if in a particular case we find it impossible, we think of this as due to some defect. It is not a defect in a kangaroo that it cannot speak fluent Hebrew, but if, as is probably the case, it is impossible for me to do so, this is because of moral and intellectual defects on my part.

Mankind is thus constituted by what at first sight look like two kinds of exchange between its members, biological exchanges and linguistic exchanges. These seem to be two ways in which we share a common life. If we came across something that seemed to share our life in only one of these ways, we should not be sure whether to call it human or not. What would we say of visitors from Mars who were able to speak with us but unable to interbreed with us ? As a matter of fact, for reasons that I shall mention later, it is by no means certain that this situation would be possible, but if it were to occur we should not be quite sure whether to describe our guests as human. On the other hand there are some 'births' which we hesitate to describe as human. The existence of natural law is due to this dual character of mankind: it is on the one hand a natural community, one that a man belongs to in virtue of his very existence, and on the other hand a linguistic community, one in which the relationship between members is a matter of language, of understanding.

Mankind thus resembles two familiar kinds of community, though it is different from each. On the one hand mankind is like any other animal species, it is a biological unity. On the other hand it is like a society, a unity constituted by conventional signs. I want now to take a look at each of these analogues to see how in each the activity of the individual is influenced or directed by his membership of the group. Since mankind is a kind of mixture of both sorts of group, this may throw light on the way in which a man's activity is influenced or directed by his membership of mankind.

If a biological species is to survive, it is necessary not merely that its members should each seek their own survival, but also that they should protect their offspring and be restrained to some extent from killing each other. The rapid developments in ethology over the past twenty years or so have taught us something about the many different techniques that have been evolved in different species to serve this end. The notion that animals other than man spend their time in indiscriminate fighting is now thoroughly discredited. Animals, of course, frequently kill members of other species, and sometimes apparently just for the fun of it, but apart from some insects and some kinds of rat, man seems to be the only animal that goes in for intra-specific violence on a really large and destructive scale. In most other species intra-specific agression has been ritualised or inhibited in one way or another. The appearance of man on the evolutionary scene did not mean, as we have sometimes supposed in the past, the introduction of reason, order and peace into a murderous jungle. It was rather the other way round; the coming of man seems to have been much more like the breakdown of a too rigid moral system; an epoch of moral bewilderment succeeding to an age of victorian morality. The taboos and inhibitions that govern the intra-specific behaviour of some other animals are exceedingly powerful. Animals that have evolved dangerous weapons that can inflict serious injury in a single attack seem also to be equipped with powerful inhibitions to prevent them from making fatal attacks on their brethren. Thus according to Konrad Lorenz, when two wolves are fighting furiously, if the vanquished one 'submits', offering his unprotected throat in a ritual gesture to the conqueror, he will not be bitten; the victorious animal is quite incapable of biting him.[1]

> In this particular situation the victor will definitely not close on his less fortunate rival. You can see he would like to but he just cannot. A dog or a wolf that offers its neck to its adversary in this way will never be bitten seriously.

There is no mystery about why this should be so; any species that lacked such a safeguard would rapidly be exterminated. Animals which are not in some way prevented from attacking their mates or their offspring don't have any descendants.[2] The direct inhibition brought into

[1] 'Konrad Lorenz, *King Solomon's Ring*, London 1954, 188.

[2] 'Among the higher vertebrates there are countless examples of such inhibitions against injuring fellow-mem-

play by a particular ritual gesture—a symbolic submission by the weaker party—is only one of the ways in which a species may be protected from itself. There are a great many other techniques, sometimes involving quite elaborate social arrangements, but it is not my business here to describe these. I have merely given one example of the way in which group membership affects the behaviour of an individual of the species. The inhibition I have been speaking of is the bearing of the whole group upon its member. The animal behaves in this way not for any reason connected with its individual requirements but because the survival of the whole group demands it. There is sometimes, as Lorenz points out, a quite visible tension between what the animal would 'like' to

bers of the species, and they often play an essential part in situations where the anthropomorphising observer would never suspect that aggression was present or that special mechanisms were necessary for its suppression. For example, to people who believe in the 'infallibility' of instinct, it will seem paradoxical that an animal mother has to be prevented, by special inhibitions, from aggressiveness towards her own children, particularly towards the newborn or newly hatched. In reality, these special inhibitions against aggression are very necessary because a brood-tending animal parent, at the time when it has young, has got to be particularly aggressive towards every other living creature.' Konrad Lorenz, *On Aggression*, London 1966, 98.

do, in terms of its own 'personal satisfaction', and what it has to do because of the needs of the group. The point I want to make immediately is that the direction from the group is transmitted to the individual genetically. The animal is born with the necessary instincts. In the purely biological community, direction by the group is genetic. If an individual shares in the life of the group biologically, it will receive its direction from the group biologically—for example in the form of an inherited inhibition. I shall be suggesting that in a parallel but contrasting way, when an individual shares in the life of the group linguistically, he will receive direction from it linguistically, in the form, for example, of rules; prohibitions will replace inhibitions. In the case of mankind, which is both biological and linguistic, there is an odd mixture of both.

Before leaving the animal species, however, there is one important point to be made. An animal species is not a mere logical class, it is a physical object. True, it is a strange kind of physical object—it does not, for example, exist all at one time—nevertheless it is an object which began to exist during some period in the past and will cease to exist some time in the future and which at any time occupies a certain amount of space. What I mean by a mere logical class is this: An observer may invent the class of red things in which would be included blood and British letter boxes and certain noses; these things have nothing in common except that someone has decided to class them together; they all interest him in one particular way. This is what I mean by a logical class. It is constituted not by any physical interaction between its members, but simply by a relationship between each of the members and an observer. Contrast this with the species of panthers. This does not exist because some scientific observer has noticed that all these animals resemble each other in certain ways, it exists because all these animals belong to each other in certain ways. The species does not exist because there are many individual animals which resemble each other; rather the contrary, any individual exists because there is a species from which it can be born. Individuals belong to a logical class by grace of the observer; they belong to a species by grace of their parents. It is fundamental to the theory of human ethics we are considering that mankind is not just a logical class but a species, constituted by relationships amongst its members. There is such an identifiable object as the species of panthers to which all panthers belong; there is no such object as the 'class of all red things' to which all red things belong. To say 'this belongs to the class of red things' is just a pompous way of saying 'this is red'. It adds absolutely nothing to what you know of an individual red thing to be told that it belongs to such a class. But 'this belongs to the species of panther' is a remark different from, and more informative than 'this is a panther'. You might say the latter without realising that there existed a species of panthers, you might think that the panther you met was a unique creation or a god, sufficient to itself, concerned only for itself. To be told that it belongs to a species is to be told not that there are others like it (there may not be; perhaps they have all been shot) but that part of what this panther is is to be a fragment of a larger whole. It is to be told that part of its behaviour is to be explained by the requirements of this larger whole. Not to know that the panther belongs to a species would be not to know something about this individual panther; membership of the species is part of what it means for the panther to be itself. It is a consequence of this that when its behaviour is influenced by its membership of the species, it is not suffering violence from outside. There may well be a tension between what it would like to do as an individual and what it has to do as a species-member, but this is a tension within the animal itself. When it acts in accordance with the inhibition, let us say, it is not submitting to some exterior force, but to a depth within itself. I am going to suggest that, in a parallel way, when a man obeys the law of his 'species', the natural law, he is being true to a depth within himself, and that to act contrary to this law is to violate himself at his centre. The tension in the wolf that is inhibited from finishing off his opponent is as physically real and obvious as if he were restrained by a chain, and yet what in fact restrains him is simply that deep down he does not want to kill. There is a struggle here between two levels of wanting; one stimulated by the immediate circumstances of the fight, the anger and the excitement, the other necessitated by the long-term needs of the wolf species as a whole. As I shall be suggesting later, human morality is entirely concerned with doing what I want to do, but in man too we have to reckon with several levels of wanting, and we can only truly do what we want, only truly be free, if we get the priorities right.

Now I want to turn to another kind of group, the linguistic community. It would be nice to be able first of all to look at a purely biological community, such as the wolves, and then turn to look at a purely linguistic community, but unfortunately things are not as neat as this. There is no such thing on earth as a purely linguistic community. Every linguistic community has biological grounds as well. The nearest approach to a purely linguistic group, a group whose whole unity depended simply on language, would I suppose be people playing some intensely intellectual game by post; some game in which there was the absolute minimum of the sort of emotional fellowship created by bridge or bingo. Certainly the political community is not simply constituted by its overt conventional signs, its laws and language and other symbols. It depends for its unity to a great extent on primitive emotions connected with territory and kinship. Nevertheless, since the notion of law belongs primarily to this political community I shall take this grouping as my example, trying to deal with it just in so far as it is a linguistic community. I want to see how the direction of the group bears upon the individual, how his behaviour is affected by the needs of the group as a whole.

First of all a word about laws and what they are not. If when I am driving along the road I come across a sign that reads 'Dangerous Bend' or one of those curiously cowardly signs that say 'Beware of Sheep', I am being given a piece of information which may help me to make good decisions about my driving. The point of such warning or informative signs is that they help me to make decisions. There is, however, another radically different kind of notice: this is the sort that reads '30'. Such a notice is a command, a piece of law. It is of course a sentence which could be re-written 'do not drive over 30 mph'. Now no doubt the sign has been erected because on this stretch of road it is usually dangerous to exceed that speed, but this is not what it says; it does not, of itself, give information, it gives a command. From the presence of this sign, together with my confidence in the good sense of the local county council, I could no doubt deduce that it would be dangerous to drive here at 60 mph, but the sign is not a sign of this information. What then does it do? In what way does it help me to drive better? The purpose, I think, of such a sign is not to help me make a decision, but to take the decision for me. There are a whole lot of decisions to be taken in driving a car and one of them concerns speed. The effect of the speed limit is that this decision has been, at least partially, taken by the county council. It is as though the county council were taking part in the driving of the car. Such a situation will arise only when the driving of my car is the concern of the community as a whole, when my car and how it is driven become part of the way in which the community live together. In a non-industrial community in which cars were rare or unimportant the community would have no need to take a hand in the driving of them.

A law such as the speed-limit is a decision affecting my activity taken in view not of my individual needs but of those of the community, and there is a clear analogy here with the inhibitions on intra-specific violence to be found in other species. In each case the purpose of the direction, whether prohibition or inhibition, is the welfare of the group as a whole. It is, of course, wildly metaphorical to speak of a mechanism developed by evolution as something whose purpose is the survival of the species, as though evolution were some kind of conscious agent. All we really mean is that the mechanism is to be found around the place *because* it has contributed to survival. There might be a more exact parallel if all county councils took decisions absolutely at random; we should find that the surviving counties had traffic laws. Most county councils, however, do not work in this way.

We now have to ask why the community's direction of my behaviour should take the form of making decisions for me. Why is it not sufficient for the community to supply me with the necessary information upon which I can make my own decisions. Why, in fact, should we have '30' signs as well as 'Dangerous Bend' signs? We need a good justification for this because the imperative form, as we shall see, has special disadvantages by comparison with the indicative form. It is less flexible and leads to what I shall call 'hard cases'. Nevertheless it could be argued that we are putting the question the wrong way round. The question ought to be 'why do we have 'Dangerous Bend' signs as well as '30' signs?' If it is really the case that some ways in which my car is used are of immediate concern to the community as a whole, if they affect the survival and welfare of the whole community rather than simply my own welfare, it is surely natural to expect decisions about them to be taken by whatever voice speaks for the community as a whole. There might be purely pragmatic reasons for, so to speak, farming out the decisions amongst the individuals, but the burden of proof would be on those who recommended this. In the United States it is alleged that there are pragmatic reasons why public services such as the telephone system or transport or the provision of medical care should be in private hands; this may well be the case, but it is clearly incumbent on those who say so to show what these reasons are. The reasons are likely to be that we get greater efficiency when we are able to make on the spot decisions rather than following some fixed rule laid down beforehand. At any rate, in the case of the traffic rules, it has been found that in our present state of industrialisation the best results are obtained by the community taking a few decisions about which side of the road to use, maximum speeds and so on, and leaving the rest to individual decision. Now we can return to our question: why not leave *everything* to individual decision? We may look briefly at three possible answers: we cannot be left to take all decisions ourselves because we are too stupid, too busy or too vicious. The first of these assumes that the county council is so much more intelligent than most people in the community that its long-distance general rule will be a more efficient means of controlling a citizen's car than would be the citizen's own decision on the spot. The second is more plausible; it points to the fact that if we had to stop and consider all the relevant facts before knowing what to do in any situation, we should have no time for living. For the third, the value of law, as distinct from information or warning, is that it can be enforced by sanctions; a large number of people simply will not be bothered to make a rational decision about their driving and so it is wise to make some of the decisions for them and compel them to obey.

While there is probably something in each of these reasons, it is worth looking for a reason for having laws which would be valid even if everyone were thoroughly rational, utterly painstaking and tediously virtuous. One such reason might be based on the need for predictability. My decisions are always taken in the context of other people's decisions and I need to be fairly sure about what these are going to be. To drive my car efficiently I must drive it amongst other drivers who are not only conscientious and courteous, but also predictable. Driving a car in a country in which there were no traffic rules at all would be a fascinating and absorbing art, also it would take a great deal of time, for there would of course be other drivers also playing the same game. (Those who have driven in Ireland will know what I mean.) The sheer delightful business of getting from one place to another with, let us say, your load of frozen fish would absorb so much of your energy and time that there would not be much left for freezing the fish, building the lorries, etc. In such a society car-driving could only be a leisure-time activity, a hobby; there would have to be some other means of actual transport. If, however, a country is so industrialised as to need cars for its survival then it will need efficient driving and this means uniformity of decision amongst drivers. If you can rely on not meeting traffic in the left lane you can travel a lot faster; if in a congested area you can rely on all the other cars travelling at about 30 then you can go at about 30 yourself; if there is the real possibility of meeting someone doing 60 then the prudent thing would be to travel at about 12 yourself. And so certain decisions about the position and speed of your car are made for everybody by the community as a whole. The 30 mph limit is not simply to force irresponsible drivers by sanctions to be responsible—it is first of all to ensure that all drivers are responsible in the same way.

This argument, however, will only really work in the case of what we might call 'arbitrary' decisions. It works, in fact, in those cases in which, so long as there is a decision, it does not matter what the decision is. So long as we all agree to travel on the same side of the road, it does not matter whether this is the left or the right. Just because it does not matter there is no way of predicting what an intelligent virtuous man will decide about it; just because of this we need a central authority to decide the matter for everyone.

We might agree, then, that in a wholly intelligent and virtuous society there would be need for regulations of this kind; it is by no means clear that there would be need for laws governing matters in which there is just one right thing to do. The most that might be needed in such cases would be information. It looks, therefore, as though, apart from such 'arbitrary' regulations as the rule of the road, laws, as distinct from information, are only required because people are to some extent stupid and vicious.

There is, however, no need to give up so quickly. Consider what 'giving information' actually involves. Once we admit that our paragons of citizens might need to be given information from some central source, then I think we will have to admit that they might just as well be given laws. What, as a matter of fact, is the reaction of the virtuous driver to a notice saying 'Dangerous Bend'? He will slow down because he makes it a rule always to do so at dangerous corners. If he makes it a rule, why should not society as a whole do so? The information conveyed by 'Dangerous Bend' is that it is usually a bad thing to drive fast at this point, that there is a risk involved, that there is a probability that normal speeds would lead to catastrophe. Now to make a decision based on such probabilities is a much trickier matter than making one based on simple facts. If I know that everyone who drinks methylated spirits dies rather soon, then it is easy to decide against drinking it; but if I know that quite *probably* if I smoke I will get lung cancer, it does not immediately follow that if I am against getting lung cancer I will be against smoking. It is quite certain that a large number of people who smoke will not get lung cancer, although a large number will. Between the information about probability and the decision there intervenes an assessment of what counts as a reasonable risk and what as an unreasonable one. Now supposing I decide not to smoke. It may well be that in fact I could have smoked without suffering any ill effects; if so I am the victim of a 'hard case' in exactly the same way as someone who has to obey a law even in the peculiar circumstances in which the reason for the law is absent—someone, for example, who has to drive at 30 even in special circumstances when there would plainly be no danger in travelling at 50.

Thus if the objection to law, as distinct from information, is that it is relatively inflexible and leads to 'hard cases', then we must admit that the same objection applies to information about probabilities. Clearly it makes no difference whether I, confronted with a warning, make my own estimate of risk and thus make a rule for myself, or whether society makes the rule for everyone: in either case I will be more restricted in my activity than I would be if I acted simply on information about the facts of this particular case. If instead of a probability statement like 'Dangerous Bend' the county council were to say 'there is an articulated truck approaching you at 37 mph around the next corner, there is a small patch of grease towards the centre of the road . . .' then I could come to my own decision quite simply. But, of course, the obvious way to make such information available would be to improve and straighten the road; a dangerous bend is just a place where such precise information is hard to come by.

In a society whose citizens were not only intelligent and virtuous but also informed of every relevant fact in every situation, there would be no need for probable statements or warning of what usually happens and similarly no need for laws. But in a society which was merely intelligent and virtuous there would be need for general statements about risks etc, and since these lead to the same kind of 'hard cases' as do laws, there seems no reason why such a society should not have laws as well—in cases where it is less bother to have the risk assessed by an expert than to have to make a rule for myself. And, of course, in a society such as our own which is not even particularly intelligent or virtuous, laws would have the added advantage of being attended by sanctions.

If this will stand as an account of why a linguistic community directs its members by means of laws, we may turn to compare such a community with mankind. Like a society, mankind, at least to some extent, finds its unity in language; can we speak of the 'laws' of mankind? We are at once, of course, confronted by an obvious difficulty: if there is to be a law, where are we to find the lawgiver? If I am not simply, after assessing the risks and probabilities, to make rules for myself, if I am to have them made for me, it would seem that I must seek somewhere for the equivalent of the county council for mankind. I do not, however, think that the notion of natural law stands or falls by the discovery of such a lawgiver. I think we could speak of natural law if I made rules for myself and then saw that these are the rules which would have been made for everybody by a 'county council' if we happened to hear its voice. The situation would be like that of a motorist who makes it a rule never to travel at more than 20 on a particularly nasty bit of road and thinks that there ought to be a speed-limit.

As a matter of fact Aquinas, though I think basically accepting this account of natural law—it is promulgated to us, he said, through our having reason—did think also that the 'county council' had spoken. He thought that God, as the inventor of mankind, the one who made the decisions about what sort of institution mankind should be, had as a matter of fact issued the basic laws of mankind as well. He thought that the ten commandments were a matter of God telling us the natural law. Now in a queer way I think Aquinas was right about this, though it would be better to put it the other way round. It is not God who reveals to us the ten commandments, but the ten commandments that reveal God to us.

In Exodus the revelation of the ten commandments occurs in the context of a theophany, a manifestation of God, and they are essentially concerned with the difference between Yahweh and the other gods. The decalogue is part of the general demystifying of the divine that lies at the centre of the Jewish-christian tradition. The other gods, the ones that Israel has beyond everything else to shun, make their demands in terms of special religious cults, but the demand of Yahweh is that men should have a certain kind of relationship with each other in the secular world. Of course the Old Testament describes a very elaborate cult of Yahweh but religious activity of this kind is always seen as subordinate to morality.[1] When Jesus insists on this point he is reiterating an Old Testament theme.

However, Aquinas, as I have said, thought of the ten commandments as a promulgation of the natural law; they were, for him, a definition of man as well as a revelation of God. A definition provided verbally by the inventor of man. Nevertheless he did not think this verbal promulgation absolutely necessary. He thought that it was possible for man with much difficulty, after a

[1] 'The lack of special cultic requirements (in the decalogue) is noteworthy. This corresponds to the fact that in the Old Testament cultic action is indeed generally presupposed as a possible, even a requisite way of worship, but that the special and unique element in the relationship between God and Israel is not evident in the cultic sphere but in the obedience to the one God and his demands which pertain to human relationships. Even the sabbath commandment is no exception here, for whatever may have been the significance of the sabbath, in the view of the decalogue it was at all events not thought of as a cultic feast.' Martin Noth, *Exodus*, London 1962, 167.

long time and with the admixture of many errors, to discover, without being told, what the natural law commands. The idea that it is easy to know the natural law or that most men may be expected to understand it or that knowledge of it is somehow innate in us is quite foreign to his thinking, but so also is the idea that we can know it only by direct divine revelation. Nothing in his theory would lead us to expect the natural law to be the highest common factor of the moral codes of different societies. Since he thought it rather hard to discover he would presumably not have been surprised to find that small primitive communities were hazy about it and held bizarre views about sexual morals or the ethics of killing —they would doubtless be equally ignorant of genetics and astro-physics. As a good aristotelian he would not have shared the romantic belief that primitive societies, being more 'natural', are in closer touch with natural law than are sophisticated and industrialised societies.

In this I think he would have been at least partially wrong. Whatever may be true of primitive societies it is at least arguable that the sophisticated society does present certain obstacles to understanding the nature of man, not, however, because it is industrialised but because it is capitalist or profoundly affected by capitalism.

As Karl Marx remarked, 'According to Adam Smith, society is a commercial enterprise. Every one of its members is a salesman. It is evident how political economy establishes an alienated form of social intercourse as the true and original form and that which corresponds to human nature'.[1] A certain distortion of the nature of man is built into the capitalist culture which makes it difficult for us to recognise ourselves for what we are, to recognise, in fact, what we *want*.

It will, I suppose, be clear that the 'natural laws', the demands made upon a man by his membership of his 'natural community', the human race, represent his own deepest desires. I think I can best explain this with the help of a passage from D. H. Lawrence in his remarkable essay *Apropos of Lady Chatterley's Lover*.

> All that matters is that men and women should do what they really want to do. Though here as elsewhere [he is discussing sex and marriage] we must remember that man has a double set of desires, the shallow and the profound, the personal, superficial, temporary

[1] 'Economic Studies from Marx's Notebooks' in *Karl Marx: Selected Writings in Sociology*, London 1963, 179.

> desires, and the inner, impersonal, great desires that are fulfilled in long periods of time. The desires of the moment are easy to recognise, but the others, the deeper ones, are difficult. It is the business of our Chief Thinkers to tell us of our deeper desires, not to keep shrilling our little desires into our ears.[1]

Ethics is entirely concerned with doing what you want, that is to say with being free. Most of the problems arise from the difficulty of recognising what we want. The penalty with which we are threatened for breaking the ethical 'law' is thus unfreedom, or 'imprisonment' by ultimately alien forces; breaking the moral law means doing what deeply we do not want to do.

Remorse differs from regret in just this respect. Regret means realising that you *now* wish you had not behaved in a certain way; remorse is the realisation that you did not really wish to behave in that way *at the time*, that the behaviour was contrary to your deepest desires, your need to be truly yourself. Remorse is much more catastrophic than regret; it is a revolutionary act in the sense that it involves a reassessment of your past, a re-writing of your autobiography. As

[1] D. H. Lawrence, *Apropos of Lady Chatterley's Lover*, London 1931, 52–53.

Lawrence points out, for a variety of reasons we are frequently unaware of ourselves until too late; we find it easy not to take into account our long-term desires but to satisfy our 'superficial, temporary desires' at their expense.

> Man has little needs and deeper needs. We have fallen into the mistake of living from our little needs till we have almost lost our deeper needs in a sort of madness. There is a little morality which concerns persons and the little needs of man; and this, alas, is the morality we live by. But there is a deeper morality, which concerns all womanhood, all manhood, and nations and races and classes of men. This greater morality affects the destiny of mankind over long stretches of time, applies to man's greater needs and is often in conflict with the little morality of the little needs.[1]

It is fairly easy to see the correspondence between these 'deeper needs' and the mechanisms of restraint which, in other animal species, ensure the long-term survival of the group. We call them mechanisms of 'restraint' only because they sometimes do come into conflict with the 'little needs' of the individual animal. In them-

[1] *Apropos*, 80.

selves they are not restraints but simply manifestations of the deep and originating species-life of the individual. Now in a similar way, the deep desires that a man has, the desires he cannot help having, are a manifestation of his human life. His being human consists in his having what Aquinas calls these 'natural inclinations'. They are the presence to him of the law of his nature, the natural law.

The natural law thus does not require a law-giver, except in the sense that we may regard our humanity as *given*. We can, however, as we come to understand mankind, construct the code of law which would have been given if there had been a law-giver; but the whole purpose of such a code is to serve as a clue to the inclinations that are within us but difficult to discern. If we write in our code the precept 'do not kill children', it is, as Lawrence says, to 'tell us of our deeper desires', to warn us that in our deepest selves we do not want to do this, that such activity will violate us at the very centre of our personality, even though we may produce several rather shrill reasons why it is the best thing to do in the situation.

The position is slightly complicated by the fact that besides these deep desires that define our humanity, we have also inherited certain deep feelings from our pre-human ancestors which to some extent overlap with our deep human desires but are not identical with them. It is important to be on our guard against what seems to be the thesis of such writers as Robert Ardrey (in his boring and pretentious but informative book *The Territorial Imperative*[1]) that nationalism, the class-structured society, private ownership, competition and, in general, all the apparatus of the political right are somehow validated by the fact that they have their roots in primitive animal instincts. For one thing this is what the left has always suspected anyway and all it shows is that such institutions are tenacious and probably cannot be destroyed by sweet reason alone. This pre-human inheritance probably accounts for a good deal of what we call our 'moral feelings'. Thus, for example, we have inherited a partial inhibition on killing each other at close quarters. If you have to stick a knife into someone you will probably feel sick unless you have worked yourself up enough or have been carefully trained. This is all very well in its way, such feelings can often be a valuable clue to what we really want, but they are too crude (the inhibition which might prevent a murder would also prevent

[1] Robert Ardrey, *The Territorial Imperative*, London 1967.

surgery) and, what is worse, they break down in the face of technology. If I show you half a dozen babies and force you to burn them alive on a fire one by one, you will certainly be sick, and very probably you will go crazy through doing violence to your inherited mechanism of inhibition. If, however, I put you in an aeroplane and make you press the button that releases the napalm which has exactly the same effect on the children below, it is quite likely that you will suffer no serious emotional ill-effects, even though you are doing something that is contrary to your deepest inclinations, something destructive of your identity.

Lawrence spoke of a conflict between the great morality and the little morality. This is what I have called the 'hard case', when the demands of my fundamental desires seem to make me act unreasonably, when one does not see any profit in behaving in accordance with them. I think that such cases are a good deal more rare than the textbooks of ethics might lead one to suppose but the fact that it predicts such situations is, to my mind, one of the many virtues of the theory of natural law. Any theory of ethics according to which moral tragedy might always be averted by more careful calculation is plainly at variance with the facts of experience. The idea that discovering and expressing our real selves, doing, as I say, what we really want to do, will result in happiness and contentment in any immediate sense is simply infantile. Yet there must be some kind of happiness or contentment at a deeper level. The use of the natural law is to say 'this is what you really want—isn't it?' You may take this to a certain extent on trust even though you are not conscious of wanting this at all, but in the end the proposal of the law must correspond to what you recognise as your real desires. We can only expect happiness when we arrive at the stage of fulfilling our deep desires not because we have been told what they are, but because we personally feel them. Such genuine freedom can only be the result of a long period of investigation into our true wants. The theory thus proposes two approaches to the question, 'what is it morally good to do?' One approach seeks, by investigating the kind of community that mankind is, to discover what its laws must be and hence what I who am by nature a member of mankind must deeply want to do; the other is a direct 'autobiographical' investigation of what I find myself wanting to do. Morals, on this theory, would be conducted as a dialectical discussion in which these two sources of illumination reflect upon each other.

The criticism I have to make of this theory of ethics as law will appear in the next chapter. Its weakness, as I see it, is its too ready assumption that mankind as a unity exists 'by nature'. It seems to me that human unity is something towards which we move, a goal of history. We need to take more seriously the truth that mankind is in one way self-creative, that since our unity is linguistic as well as biological, it is not simply given to us but also made by us.

# 3
# Ethics as language

Man is the linguistic animal. When we say this we are not just pointing to a distinguishing characteristic of man—as if we might say 'giraffes are the ones with the long necks, men are the ones that talk'. Language does not only distinguish man from other animals, it distinguishes his animality from that of other animals. To be a man is to be an animal in a new sense, to be alive in a new sense. This means that even the activities which a man seems to share with other animals are transfigured by the fact that they are part of an animality that finally issues in language. Man does not just *add* speech on to such things as eating and sexual behaviour; the fact that these latter occur in a linguistic context makes a difference to what they are.

Language is a culmination of organic life. In

order to give an account of any organism we have to use words like 'relevance' and 'significance'. A structure counts as an organism when the activities of the parts have to be understood in terms of their relevance to the whole—what goes on in the eye is called 'seeing' because of the part it plays in the activity of the animal as a whole. Of course we can talk about very simple organisms without bringing in such notions as relevance, we can talk about them in the same way that we talk about simple machines. Similarly we can talk about sufficiently complicated machines as though they were animals: 'the computer tries out various solutions . . . searches through its data . . . .' It is difficult to say what makes us decide between using 'animal language' and using 'machine language', between regarding this thing as alive or not. It is difficult because there is plainly no single reason; there are a great many considerations to be taken into account. The point is that if we do decide to talk of something as organic, then we employ a whole family of terms that have to do with significance and relevance.

The dog sees the meat as food, as having a certain significance for its life. I do not, of course, mean that the dog says to itself 'this is food', but it shows its appreciation of it as food by trying to eat it. Of course you could describe all that, if you wanted to, in terms of certain successive chemical reactions and physical movements, you could describe it as though the dog were a machine, using chemists' and physicists' language. If you did this you would not use words like 'food', 'trying' or 'eating'. Such a programme would seem forced and unnatural and, in its way, just as whimsical as talking in organic terms about cars and trains: 'she made a heroic effort up the gradient but expired before she got to the top'. There was a time when people assigned a special status to the language of the chemist and physicist, so that it was felt to be somehow more virtuous to suppress our natural way of talking about dogs and grimly to speak of them as though they were machines. This particular piece of prudery—known as 'materialism'—is, I am glad to say, no longer with us. There are, of course, a whole range of borderline cases in which we are not sure whether to use the language of organism or of machine; when we ask 'is this a living thing or not?' Since, however, these are precisely the cases where either language will do equally well, it is hard to see why there should be any fuss about the matter.

To get back to the dog. He sees certain kinds of stuff in the light of food, and he sees various other things in various other lights, as dangerous, or sexually exciting, or repulsive or whatever. In other words he sees significance in his environment. He is not surrounded by neutral facts but by things that matter to him in various ways. He has a *world*. By a world I mean an environment organised in terms of significance. What we call the senses of the dog are the ways in which this organisation takes place. We know a certain amount about the world of the dog; we know that it differs a good deal from our world. Colour, for example, has no significance for a dog, it does not exist in his world. On the other hand, as everyone knows, in comparison with dogs we haven't got no noses. The world of a dog may be as exciting or boring in terms of smell as ours can be in terms of colour.

Senses, then, are modes of response to an environment or modes of determining a world. The senses are not eyes and ears and other bits of an animal, they are what the animal is doing with these bits or, if you like, the way in which the behaviour of these bits is relevant to the behaviour of the whole body. Hearing is how my whole body lives through my ears, walking is how it lives through my legs, eating is how it lives through my mouth and stomach and so on. The bodily structure of an animal will determine how it constitutes a world from its environment, but the transaction is not completely unilateral, important environmental changes affect the animal's world and eventually, by natural selection, the bodily structure. But broadly speaking we can say that an animal is an area of sensual life, a point from which a world is organised.

We may ask at this point about the 'environment' which lies behind the animal's world. Is it correct to think of an objectively real environment waiting to be organised into worlds by different animals? The animal is plainly enclosed within its sensual system; it cannot be aware of an environment except as organised into a world by its sensuous life. If we speak of an environment 'behind' the animal's world we are speaking simply of *our* world. We are not, however, simply being provincial in giving a special status to our world, because it is created not simply by sensuous life but by linguistic life; and language, as we shall see, is precisely a way of not being a prisoner of the sensuous life. The linguistic animal is the one that to some extent creates its own modes of response to the environment, its own modes of constituting a world, and to this extent is not their prisoner.

But to return to the animals. Each animal is the centre of a world, it is an area of sensuous activity that constitutes a world from the environment. Actively sharing a common world is communication. I say 'actively', because any two animals with the same sensory apparatus could be said to share a common world—we have already spoken of 'the world of the dog', which is shared by all dogs—but two dogs are in communication when they are actively engaged together in the determination of a common world. Communication is actively sharing a common life.

Discussion of communication amongst animals is too often confined to the means by which bits of information are conveyed from one to another, but this is simply a piece of anthropomorphism. Amongst men there is an important distinction between the exchange of messages and the other ways of communicating. We distinguish between conversation and choral singing, though both are forms of communication; still more do we distinguish between conversation and common work, though again we have here two kinds of communication. In the pre-linguistic world of the other animals these distinctions have no real place: the bee that dances 'to show the others where the honey is' is no more (and no less) communicating with its fellow bees than when it shares their life in other ways. To single out the dance of the bees or the call of a bird from the rest of its vital activity is to project onto the pre-linguistic world a distinction that only properly has place amongst men.

All shared vital activity is, then, some form of communication. We may speak of the vital response of an animal to its environment as a kind of communication. The animal vitalises its world and endows it with significance. The world becomes the clothing of the animal and, in a way, an extension of its body. We can see this dramatically in the case of those animals that have a certain personal territory. Here the boundaries of the territory are almost like another skin; the violence with which the animal reacts to penetration of its territory is comparable to the convulsion that occurs when a weapon enters the skin. The space around such an animal has begun to share in its bodily life.

I have spent time on communication and animal life in order to lay a foundation for the use of the word when we come to the linguistic animals. In man communication reaches a new intensity, it becomes language. I think it is important to see language not first of all in terms of the operation that is peculiar to it—the transfer of messages—but to see it as a mode of communication, a sharing of life. With the appearance of language we come, in evolution, to one of those radical changes that I mentioned earlier; a change in which we do not merely see something new but have a new way of seeing; in which something is produced which could not be envisaged in the old terms and which changes our whole way of envisaging what has gone before. The coming of this new kind of communication, this new way of being alive, could not, so to speak, have been predicted before it happened. It is only after it has happened that, looking back in the new terms, from the standpoint of the new kind of life, we can see the continuity of previous life with this. We can then see that, as Aquinas puts it, 'understanding is a kind of living; it is, indeed, the most perfect kind of living'.

We sometimes play with the question 'could we make a machine that talks?' This is to ask whether we could give an account wholly in 'machine language' of something which would then turn out to be a linguistic being—this is what would be required if we were to have a technique for making one. The significant question to ask here, however, is 'what would count as success; what would make us say that we had before us a talking being?' The answer, surely, is that we would say we had a talking being when we recognised that it was talking *to* us. Nothing that we know *about* the thing can compel such a recognition on our part. I think that an important factor here would be irony. We would come to recognise an intelligent response as we detected ironic overtones in the machine's remarks; but the nature of irony and its detection is too complex a subject for us to consider for the moment. We can only say that when the machine begins to talk (when it becomes free and intelligent and enters into human communication) it will announce the fact itself and we will either believe it or not. The change required of us here, from knowing the thing as an object—knowing things about it—to responding to it as another subject, corresponds to the radical change from pre-linguistic to linguistic.

We must now try to characterise the new kind of communication that is language. I think the central point is that with the linguistic animal the media of communication are created by the animal itself. We do not just communicate with each other, we create the means by which we communicate. We do not simply use such tools as we have to make things, we make the tools themselves. The communication of other animals is a matter of shared sensuous life, and the forms of this life are determined by their sensory apparatus, by the kind of bodies they have. A dog has a definite kind of world, which it can share with other dogs, because it has a definite bodily structure. Its life and its world is determined by the constitution of its sensory organs. The human body, on the other hand, is not only more complex than that of other animals but in its extension into its world, in the kind of communication media that surround it, it is to some extent self-determinative. We can communicate in media that we invent ourselves, in language; the media of other animals are genetically determined.

There are several qualifications to be made to that statement: as we shall see, we do not and cannot individually create our own media of expression except in a very marginal sense, moreover it is not quite true that in other animals the media of communication are unalterably fixed. Konrad Lorenz states quite flatly:

> Of course this purely innate signal code of an animal species differs fundamentally from human language, every word of which must be learned laboriously by the human child. Moreover, being a genetically fixed character of the species—just as much as any bodily character—this so-called language is for every individual animal species ubiquitous in its distribution.

> Obvious though this fact may seem, it was nevertheless with something akin to naive surprise that I heard the jackdaws in northern Russia 'talk' exactly the same familiar 'dialect' as my birds at home in Altenberg.[1]

H. Munro Fox, however, records a rather charming minor exception to this rule:

> The song of the chaffinch in Switzerland is distinctly different from that in England, and the song is slightly different in various parts of Britain. On the Continent chaffinches migrate long distances . . . it so happens that a stream of continental migrants passes annually along the Essex coast and from them the native birds acquire a continental accent.[2]

There are of course quite well known cases of imitative learning by birds and other animals and if, as I have suggested, it is merely an anthropomorphic mistake to treat the 'signal codes' of animals as something specially distinct from the rest of their bodily behaviour, we must include here all sorts of 'learning' with regard to other kinds of activity. It is, in principle, no more surprising that birds should learn new songs by

[1] *King Solomon's Ring*, 76.

[2] H. M. Fox, *The Personality of Animals*, London 1952, 28.

imitation than that the cat should learn to manipulate the door latch; neither more nor less communication is involved.

Lorenz is particularly insistent on the gulf between animal signals and human language. There is, he says, no question of any animal having the conscious intention of influencing another when it makes the appropriate sign. Speaking of some of the most 'communicative' of birds, he says:

> Even geese and jackdaws, when reared singly make all these signals as soon as the corresponding mood overtakes them. Under these circumstances the automatic and even mechanical character of these signals becomes strikingly apparent and reveals them as entirely different from human words.[1]

We have then to see language both as the culmination of a developing process of communication, the most intense kind of communication, but also as quite different from all that has gone before; the root of the difference being that other animals are born with their systems of communication, whereas for children the entry into language is a personal matter, a matter of their own biography.

[1] *King Solomon's Ring*, 77.

There are, as I see it, three major factors in the growth of human media of communication: nature, history and biography. By nature I mean what we are immediately born with; the structure of our sensory apparatus which is, of course, genetically determined. Our linguistic communication grows out of our sensuous communication. Our linguistic life (human life) is not determined by the structure of our sense organs in the way that the life of other animals is, but it depends upon it. In order to learn the language of a wholly strange people it is necessary to live with them, to share their efforts and disappointments and pleasures, their daily way of life. Then by imitation we come to use their language appropriately, we discover the use of their various sounds. We learn by our mistakes, recognising a mistake by the fact that it makes a barrier between ourselves and the community, impeding our conformity to their way of life. This, roughly speaking, is how children learn their 'native' language. Now being able to share a way of life with people depends on a general similarity of bodily structure. In so far as a people differed from us in, for example, the things that gave them pleasure or saddened them, still more if they differed altogether in the bodily expression of such emotions, we should find it hard to live into their community. Learning to live with strangers is, you might say, a matter of adopting the rhythms of their life, like a tuning fork vibrating in harmony with a note on the piano. Our bodies must be more or less tuned to those of the strangers in order for this to happen. It is true that we are, so to speak, self-adjusting tuning forks to a certain extent, but our range of adjustment is not indefinite, our capacity for sympathy (in the literal sense) has limits. This, I think, is why Wittgenstein said 'if a lion could talk, we could not understand him'.[1] He may have been underestimating the extent to which ethologists have succeeded in entering into the lives of lions, but his principle is surely correct; we learn a language only in so far as we can communicate in a sensuous life.[2]

Human communication, then, has its roots in

[1] L. Wittgenstein, *Philosophical Investigations*, Oxford 1953, 223e.

[2] The question is sometimes raised, though I think not often enough, about communication between men and beings from outer space who may be supposed to have entirely different bodily shapes. It is sometimes suggested, I think mistakenly, that we could find a common ground for communication on the basis of pure mathematics. This, I think, overlooks the difficulty we should have in knowing whether we were actually communicating with another linguistic being or merely with a computer.

sensuous communication although it is not determined by this. I said earlier that any animal is a centre of significance, a point from which a world is determined. When we come to human life we come to a creature that to some extent creates the significance that it gives to its world, a creature that to some extent creates its world because it creates its language.[1] For a dog, because of the determinate character of its sensuous life, a certain part of the environment will always have the significance of food. With man this is not true even of so sensuous a matter as food. Fashions in what counts as food vary from age to age and from society to society. The significance of human food is very largely created by men. For all animals, eating is a part of the business of communication; for man it is part of language. (The recognition of this, incidentally,

[1] 'Speech, of course, is the most conspicuous human achievement; speech, that is, as a structure of symbols, which again can be developed, manipulated, interpreted and re-interpreted in an infinity of directions—unlike the code of the bees, which, however marvellously complex and effective, functions as a system of fixed signals. Human language, by contrast, becomes itself a growing world of meanings within meanings, which we not only use for practical ends but dwell in as the very fabric of our being, while at the same time changing it by our participation in it, enacting the history of our language in our history.' Marjorie Grene, *The Knower and the Known*, London 1966, 174.

lies behind some recent re-statements of catholic eucharistic theology.)

What counts as food varies between broad limits set by the bodily structure of man; what brings about these variations is the second factor I mentioned, and the most important one: history. Language is the product of the community and not of the individual. In one way this is obvious enough; the English language existed before I was born and I grew into it, just as mankind existed before I was born and I came into existence as the product of it. The process of growing up, of becoming oneself, is a matter of entering into communication in terms of the various media available. This is true at every level; food, for example, is, at one level, a medium of exchange between my body and its environment; eating is a sensuous response to my world, it is one of the ways in which I constitute my world and, obviously enough, one of the ways in which I continue to live. How I grow up or how I continue to live depends in clear ways on what food is available. Eating is also a social ritual, it is a medium of exchange between members of the community, it has meaning, it is part of language. How I grow into the society, how I am able to realise myself as a part of this society again depends on the quality of the medium, on the meanings that are available. The question 'what do you eat?' fades into the question 'what does eating mean in your community' as we bring linguistic communication out of sensuous communication.

Meanings, then, are ways of entering into social life, ways of being with each other. The kind of meanings available in the language of a society—taking 'language' in its widest extent to include all conventionally determined signs and symbols—constitute the way in which people are with each other in that community. 'To imagine a language,' as Wittgenstein says, 'is to imagine a form of life.'

This way of seeing meaning and language has to be contrasted with the very widespread view based on a dualistic theory of man. According to that theory a man inhabits two worlds, an interior private world of subjectivity into which we penetrate by introspection, and an exterior public world of physical objects. These two spheres are variously called 'soul and body' or 'mind and matter' or 'thinking substance and extended substance'. The interior mind is the home of concepts and it is where thinking takes place; actions, however, words, and other expressions of my thinking take place in the public world of the body. My words consist of public signs that stand for private thoughts.

This dualism has always had a certain fatal attraction for christians; partly, I think, because the christian sees man as in tension, as torn between conflicting poles, and this theory seems to accord well with such a picture. It was deliberately and explicitly attacked from within the christian church by Aquinas in the thirteenth century, but rapidly re-asserted itself. In our own time it has come again under fire not only amongst philosophers associated with Wittgenstein, but also amongst some continental writers; there have also in recent years been attempts to show that the biblical view of man is non-dualistic. I am not, for the moment, concerned with the dualist theory in general, but only with the theory of meaning associated with it.

According to this theory concepts are generated privately in the mind and then they may or may not have words attached to them as labels. Thus I have used the word 'red' as the sign of my concept of *red*. It is one of the quirks of this theory that, since concepts are private and words are public, a real question seems to arise whether everybody who uses the word 'red' has attached it to the same concept. The empiricist kind of dualist will put the question in the form 'but how do we know that everyone who speaks of red really has the same *experience* of redness?' for to him the concept of red is a kind of experience or arises out of an experience of red things. Since the theory gives rise to a question which according to the same theory it is in principle impossible to answer, we may question the validity of the theory itself. Such problems dissolve once we recognise that what we call concepts are nothing like experiences but are simply skills in the use of words. My having the concept of *red* is nothing but my ability to use the word 'red' in the English language, in order to communicate with others. If I am satisfied that Fred and I use the word 'red' in exactly the same way, then I have already established that we have the same concept of red. This latter view, however, involves a rejection of the dualistic account. Instead of saying that I have a private mind and a public body, a mind for having concepts in and a body for saying and hearing words, I say that I have a body that is able to be with other bodies not merely by physical contact but by linguistic communication. Having a soul is just being able to communicate; having a mind is being able to communicate linguistically.

The meaning of a word, then, is the purpose it serves in the communication between people in a certain community. The question of meaning is not a question about my secret thoughts but about the public language. This is not to deny that I can have secret thoughts: of course I can. It is just to deny that they have any special position of privilege and especially to deny that thought begins in secrecy. We learn how to think by learning to use the media of communication provided by our society. Besides speaking aloud we can also imagine ourselves speaking without actually making any sound; we can talk to ourselves in our heads or imagine ourselves using other symbols. Just as after learning to read aloud we later learn to read silently, so we learn eventually to think silently. As we grow older we realise that this is quite often the best thing to do.

Meanings, then, belong first of all to the language, to the community who live by this language; the individual learns these meanings, acquires these concepts, by entering into the language, the culture or history of his community. But this, of course, is not the whole story. Communities and their languages change and develop. If we could give no account of novelty in language we should have to regard cultures as something like the fixed species of pre-evolutionary thought; forms of life that had been created from the beginning and which could only change by decaying and disappearing. The difference between a minority language which is 'dead', like Latin, which has to be kept in existence by special preservatives (and in certain schools by physical violence) and one which is alive, like Irish, is, of course, that the latter is in actual use as a medium of creative communication and especially of poetry. It is by this constant creation of new meanings or modifications of old meanings that a language remains alive. Latin, on the other hand, is used only for certain ecclesiastical communications.

Before going on to look at this third factor in the development of language, the creation of new meanings, which I have called biography, I would like to draw attention to the quasi-objective status of meaning. If we reject the dualist view that meanings are secret thoughts in my head, then we must give them a certain status which is, in important ways, independent of my will. I can't just mean what I like by words. I cannot assent to legislation that discriminates between people on grounds of race and secretly make the assent mean that I believe in a racially equal society. I can of course simply tell lies; I can not mean what I say, but I cannot, simply by taking thought, change the meaning of what I say. So meanings are, so to speak, objective, though not in the way that physical objects are. A word has a certain meaning and a piece of metal has a certain temperature and neither of these are immediately changed by anything going on in my head, though the former may eventually be modified through certain things that I do or say. I stress this point since, as will become clearer later, I think that moral values are objective in the same way as meanings and, indeed, are the meanings of behaviour.

I have spoken of the language of the community as though there were simply one society within which a man has his existence. In fact we live our lives in terms of many communities which constantly develop and dissolve. I do not only belong to the English community; I belong to a small community of friends and acquaintances; I belong to a community of people who share certain of my beliefs about political matters, and so on. These communities have each their languages; they are each contexts within which new meanings develop as new forms of relationship are discovered. The poet discovers in his experience—that is, in the community he forms with perhaps one or two others, perhaps many—new forms of communication which he can offer to the larger community who use the language.

Such an offer may be accepted or rejected as meaningless. If it is accepted he enriches the whole language, but such marginal enrichment depends on a general stability of meaning, a cultural tradition. Man's creativity is such that no traditional interpretation of the world is final; he reaches always beyond the language he has created, towards a future which, just because its language does not yet exist, can be only dimly perceived. This means that every language is in the end provisional, or at least can be seen by hindsight to have been provisional.

All animal life, then, is a matter of communication, of creating a significant world out of an environment. In the case of man this communication reaches the point of being linguistic, that is to say, man is able to some extent to create the media through which he makes his world significant. These media have their roots in the sensuous life of man and their creation is the history of a community leading into biographies, which are themselves the histories of minor communities.

It is because I have this sort of body, a human body living with a human life, that my communication can be linguistic. The human body is a source of communication; we must be careful not to think of it as an instrument used in communication like a pen or a telephone; such instruments can only be used because there is a body to use them. If the human body itself were an instrument we should have to postulate another body using it—and this, indeed, is what the dualistic theory really amounts to; the mind or soul is thought of, in practice, as a sort of invisible body living inside the visible one. Instead of this we should recognise that the human body is intrinsically communicative. Human flesh, the stuff we are made of, the intricate structure of the human organism, is quite different from wood and stone or even from animal flesh, because it is self-creative. It does not simply produce other bodies which are its children in its own image, it produces *itself* at least to the extent of creating the media, the language and communication systems which are an extension of itself.

It is not just that the human body can produce speech and writing: all its behaviour is in some degree linguistic. The range of bodily activity that we call a man's 'behaviour' consists of those actions which are significant in this way. We would not ordinarily speak of a man's digestion of his food or his tripping over a stone as his behaviour. We call a man's activity his 'behaviour' when it plays a part in his communication with others. A piece of human behaviour is not simply an action that gets something *done*, it also has meaning, it gets something *said*. I do not mean by this that all human activities are gestures. Gestures are visual words and I do not want to suggest that we are constantly talking to each other, in a literal sense, whenever we do anything. When I say that all our behaviour *says* something, I simply mean that it plays a part in some system of communication.

Now ethics is just the study of human behaviour in so far as it is a piece of communication, in so far as it says something or fails to say something. This does not mean that ethics is uninterested in behaviour in so far as it gets something done, that ethics is not concerned with the consequences of my acts, but its precise concern is with my action as meaningful. The two, of course, are closely related. It is because of the *effect* on you of having a knife stuck into you that my act of knifing you has the *meaning* that it has. But the connection may be quite loose. A mother may smack her child very lightly and almost painlessly and the child will show that he recognises the act as meaning some kind of rejection; on the other hand, in a game you may hit him much harder and he will be delighted by the sheer physical contact that means the opposite of rejection. The link between physical effect and meaning may be quite loose, but the looser it gets the nearer the action comes to being a gesture whose meaning is conventionally determined in an individual society. A painless smack may be a *gesture* of rejection, cutting a man's throat is a good deal less ambiguous.

It is because human behaviour is intrinsically meaningful that fears of committing the 'naturalistic fallacy' are beside the point. The 'fallacy' is said to consist in moving straight from factual description to value judgement, moving, as the slogan has it, from 'is' to 'ought'. No simple account of what is the case can logically entail anything that ought to be the case; or, as we might say, no account of a situation in physicist's language can entail an account in moralist's language. I think that this doctrine is an irrelevance because an account of human behaviour as such is never in physicist's language. To say that Fred killed Charlie is to say something of a quite different kind from 'this particle moved from point p at time $T_1$ to point q at time $T_2$'. To describe an event as a killing is already to describe it in terms of its significance; it is to describe it as having place in a field of communication and not simply in a gravitational or electro-magnetic field.[1] A physicist's account of Fred's action will not entail a moralist's account but neither will it entail that Fred is *killing* Charlie, just as no physicist's account of the activity of the visitor from outer space will entail that it is speaking to me.

Ethics, I have suggested, is the study of human behaviour as communication. I do not mean by this that we are concerned with human behaviour in so far as it bears on the business of talking—a man is not a bad man simply because he speaks or writes badly; for speech and writing are only part of total communication which involves the whole business of living. I am not saying that ethics is an *extension* of literary criticism, but that it is *parallel* to it. Ethics does for the whole of life what literary criticism does for a small part.

Ethics is traditionally and almost universally supposed to be concerned with the difference between right and wrong, between good and bad

[1] 'Only by an evaluation do we call the Eroica 'music', not noise, and so assimilate the 'fact' of its composition to the history of music rather than to acoustics. Only by an evaluation do we call the story of Auschwitz or Belsen mass murder and so assimilate it to human history rather than to chemistry or population genetics.' Marjorie Grene, *The Knower and the Known*, 160. The whole of this chapter on 'Facts and Values' is of very great interest.

behaviour. This is, however, a mistake: the same kind of mistake as thinking that literary criticism is concerned with the difference between good and bad poems. It is true that a man may not be thought to have got very far in his literary studies if he does not conclude that some poems are better than others, if, indeed, he does not conclude that some poems are simply atrocious; but this is not the purpose of literary criticism. Its purpose is to enable us to enjoy the poems more by responding to them more sensitively, by entering more deeply into their significance. If we try to do this we shall find that quite a lot of what is offered as poetry will not stand up to being taken as seriously as this; it is these poems that we reject as bad. Now the purpose of ethics is similarly to enable us to enjoy life more by responding to it more sensitively, by entering into the significance of human action. Here too we shall often find behaviour that does not stand up to being taken as seriously as this. There is a kind of case to be made out against literary studies in that the fastidious reader becomes incapable of enjoying certain kinds of sentimental or otherwise feeble writing. There is a similar, and equally invalid, case to be made out against the moralist. In either case the answer is too obvious to be worth stating.

There are, however, at least two important objections to the parallel between ethics and literary criticism. 'The purpose of ethics is to enable us to enjoy life.' The word 'enjoy' may seem peculiarly inappropriate in a world containing, amongst other things, Vietnam, but I use the word in the sense in which one can be said to enjoy *King Lear* or, for that matter, St Matthew's gospel. A more serious objection is that the word 'enjoy' might suggest a spectator's attitude; it might suggest that the moralist is one who stands apart from a piece of human behaviour and coolly savours it without becoming himself involved. In fact, it is impossible to appreciate the significance of human behaviour unless one is to some extent involved in it—but then surely the same should be said of our appreciation of a poem or a novel.

There is one extremely important similarity between ethics and literary criticism and this is that neither of them come to an end. I mean that, except in the case of something that can be fairly quickly dismissed as atrocious, you would not claim to have said the last word about a poem. The literary judgement is a matter of continually probing into the depths of a work, seeking a more profound understanding—an understanding which is not just of this poem but of yourself and of your world. You do not at any point say 'well, now I have understood it, there is no more to be said. I see it now precisely as a poem, in the light of literary principles, and my judgement is as follows. . . .' Now it seems to me that the same is true of ethical understanding. We should not expect to be able to say 'now I see this precisely in the light of moral principles, and my definitive judgement is as follows. . . .' We may, of course, say definitively that some behaviour is plainly atrocious, just as we may dismiss some poetry as not worth wasting time on, and in the same way we may say definitively that some action is good. But to say that a piece of human behaviour is 'good' may be as irrelevant a remark as saying that *King Lear* is good.

So I want to say that there is no such thing as *the* moral level. Moral judgement does not consist in seeing something at 'the moral level' or 'in the light of morality'; it consists in the process of trying to see things always at a yet deeper level. Moral judgement does not cease when it arrives at 'the morality of an action', it just is the continuing quest for what we might call greater seriousness or deeper understanding.

I must now try to explain what I mean by the word 'deeper' here. To say that our behaviour has significance is to say that it plays its part in some system of communication, some structure of meaning. Now we live out our lives in terms of many such structures. The quest for the 'deeper' meaning of a piece of behaviour is the quest for the part it plays in structures that are more fundamental to human existence. The view that we looked at in the last chapter is that there is one ultimate structure, one final community to which all men belong and into which all other communities are resolved, membership of mankind. The deepest meaning of an action, on this theory, is the meaning it has in terms of this system of communication. My reason for, in the end, rejecting this view is that if we take seriously the notion of mankind as a structure of meaning, as distinct from a merely biological structure, then we have to admit that it does not yet exist. Mankind is, in a sense, a theoretical construction; we argue 'if all these particular human institutions are all *human* institutions, there must be, behind them all, the institution of simply being human'. We are reminded of the kind of thinking that Wittgenstein attacks 'if all these are games there must be some concept of game that applies to them all'. In fact, for reasons discussed in the next chapter, mankind does not form a single linguistic community and this implies a defect of human communication not only in extension but also in intensity. The fact that mankind is split into fragments which are in imperfect communication with each other means that within these fragments, too, full communication is not achieved. Because I cannot express myself to all men I cannot fully give myself to any.

We do not, then, have some ultimate community within which all lesser groupings are contained, but we do have a certain hierarchy amongst the structures to which we belong. We can see that behaviour which makes sense at one level makes less sense as we move down through more fundamental forms of human relatedness or human existence. Men belong to each other (and thereby exist) in trivial ways and in less trivial ways; and even though we have to reject the natural law attempt to describe a *least* trivial way upon which the ultimate judgement of the significance of behaviour is founded, we can say that ethics is the quest of less and less trivial modes of human relatedness. In this quest ethics points towards, without being able to define or comprehend, an ultimate medium of human communication which is beyond humanity and which we call divinity. 'He who does not love does not know God; for God is love' (1 Jn 4:8)

Any piece of human behaviour has meaning at some level, however trivial it may be, otherwise we should not call it 'behaviour'. As Aquinas would put it, every human act is done for the sake of some good. We may find an activity quite meaningful at, say, the level of economics—that structure of relationship between men in which the language of money plays a large part—but as we seek to interpret it at other levels we may find it begins to fade into senselessness and non-living. A shallow cliché-ridden piece of journalese is a piece of faded language; the linguistic intensity has slackened, the texture of meaning has worn thin. In a piece of bad writing a man has not lived into his medium, you get no sense of vigorous presence. Now what the literary judgement is to writing, the ethical judgement is to the whole complex field of human communication. In some activities a man has not lived into his medium, his action has made sense at some superficial level of meaning but it does not make full human sense.

Evil behaviour may be colourfully atrocious, it may have catastrophic (and even, incidentally, good) effects on human history, but what makes us call it evil is that its meaning fades relatively soon when we try to take it seriously. The life of the evil man has meaning only at a fairly superficial level. It is entirely appropriate that Hitler's table-talk should have been so boring. Bad, cheap behaviour devalues the structures of human meaning in the way that bad cheap prose devalues the language. There is an appearance of communication concealing a failure to express oneself, to give and realise oneself. If I am right in saying that life is constituted by communication then such behaviour diminishes life or diminishes my existence. The point of evil is that it is a deprivation of reality.

Self-expression is almost the exact opposite of self-assertion. The latter substitutes domination for communication. Through fear of becoming vulnerable to others by opening ourselves to them in communication, we seek to control them so that they fit into our own world. Communication disturbs our present world, lays it open to influence from others, which may involve revolutionary change; we may prefer to tailor others to fit our familiar patterns of living. As so often in morals we can see this pattern most clearly in the behaviour of political communities. Colonialism, however mildly paternalistic (and very often the missionary activity that accompanies it), is almost the exact opposite of communication between two cultures.

There is, I think, a quite interesting distinction

to be made in almost all our media of communication between self-assertive behaviour which simply *involves* a devaluation of the medium, and the worse behaviour in which the devaluation of the medium is actually used as a *means* of self-assertion and domination. It is clear that one of our fundamental media of communication is the human body itself. Indeed it is, as we have seen, not simply an instrument but the source of all human communication. Certain kinds of physical violence, and of course killing, mean a devaluing of the body; they involve treating another's body simply as an object in my world and ignoring its status as a source of communication. But compare these activities with torture, in which the body is reduced to object status precisely for the purpose of domination; we are right, it seems to me, to judge that this is a worse activity than killing even though in the end it does the victim less harm. We are right, that is, to think that though killing is worse than hurting, torture is worse than either. In general I think the direct attack on the medium itself is more sinister than the incidental devaluation of it: as refusing to tell a man what he has a right to know is bad, but lying is worse; as theft is bad but forgery is worse. . . .

Morals in practice, then, is the attempt to live

out our lives in terms not only of the more obvious but also of the deeper forms of communication with others—we may see here a parallel with D. H. Lawrence's 'deeper desires' that I mentioned in the last chapter. Morals as a theoretical study would be the examination of these media of communication and of the relationships between them, and in this matter we probably get more help from novelists and dramatists and perhaps preachers than we do from philosophers.

# 4
# The word as law

In the last two chapters we have been looking at mankind as having or as on the way to having a certain kind of unity which is both genetic and linguistic, a unity that resembles on the one hand that of any other animal species and on the other hand that of a society. I now want to consider mankind from the point of view of dramatic unity: has the history of mankind got anything like the kind of unity through time that you get in a novel or a play? Is there such a thing as the history of man, or is there only the history of this or that culture? Is there some overall pattern in the story of man into which lesser patterns can be fitted?

A previous generation found a kind of pattern in the idea of progress; you could ask about some bit of history, let us say the crusades or the industrial revolution or the fall of Babylon, whether and to what extent it furthered or hampered the long slow march of mankind towards Mr Jeremy Thorpe. Biography and local history were all seen as parts of history which, moreover, was itself part of evolution which was probably part of God. That particular interpretation of human affairs really belongs to the world before the concentration camps, the world of Teilhard de Chardin. It was shaken by the revelation of the possibilities of human evil displayed by nazism but I think it only finally collapsed when faced by a single appalling fact: this is the fact that in various holes in the ground the government of the United States hides enough in the way of nuclear weapons to extinguish all animal life on the planet. Mankind has now definitively come of age; we can be as gods, we are for the first time in real control of our own history—we can stop it tomorrow. Making it that there should be no such thing as man is not, perhaps, quite so godlike an act as inventing man in the first place, but it belongs to the same order of things. The older kind of critic of the myth of progress used sometimes to suffer from the delusion that life was pleasanter in the past than in the present; the newer kind of critic merely questions the inevitability of any future at all.

The other great attempt to see a pattern in history is, of course, the marxist one. This certainly has the edge on the liberal progressive view in that it takes conflict more seriously and gives a more coherent account of the horrors in the world, but the marxist too must, I think, be disconcerted by the bomb. There is an element of absurdity about it that transcends any theoretical account. In a sense, total nuclear war would not be an event within history, it would be the dissolution of all history. There exist a few men whose overall behaviour is, of course, like everyone else's, conditioned by the values and interests of their class, whose general life pattern can fairly confidently be predicted in these terms. But with these men, as with everyone else, such conditioning does not extend to every detail of what they do. It is a statistical rather than a mechanical determination. Any particular small group of men might do just anything in any particular week, though the class pattern would re-establish itself in the long run. Nuclear technology means that we can no longer rely on long runs. It means that eccentric activity during just a few days on the part of a quite small group of men could bring history to a stop. When I speak of eccentricity I am not thinking of Dr Strangelove, of men becoming in the ordinary sense mad.

I am thinking of, say, Mr Barry Goldwater. Of course if Mr Goldwater had come to power he would (like Mr Reagan in California) fairly soon have been tamed to serve the real interests of neo-capitalism; but the point is that fairly soon is not soon enough. In the meantime disaster could happen. It is given to these men, not outstandingly wicked, certainly not outstandingly foolish, not just to make their contribution to the course of human history but to wield power over it. No such devastating power to ruin the whole human race has ever been in the hands of a small group of ordinary half-honest, half self-seeking politicians and soldiers since the crucifixion of Jesus Christ. A generation ago it was quite generally felt amongst educated people that one of the things that really disqualified christianity as a serious account of man was the ridiculously provincial idea that the events of a few hours on a hill outside Jerusalem could be of significance for the whole of human history. Let us by all means admit that Jesus of Nazareth played a startlingly large part in history but the christians make an absurdly larger claim. I think our present generation cannot feel quite the same, for we know that the events of a few hours on a slope outside Washington, where the Pentagon is, could undoubtedly have this total significance.

The crucifixion of Christ transforms the problem of ethics—the problem of taking human behaviour seriously—into the problem of sin and holiness. In this chapter and the next I shall try to give some account of this.

I have suggested earlier that the appearance of man on the evolutionary scene did not mean the emergence of reason and order out of a wild untamed jungle; on the contrary it was much more like the breakdown of a too rigid, too conventionalised society. The simple moral certainties of the pre-human animal world, the clear inhibitions, the fixed social structures have broken down and the new animal is faced with a much more complex world in which the traditional behaviour patterns are not much help.[1] It must have been only by a very gradual process that communication began to play a larger and larger part in the lives of the first linguistic animals. The

[1] 'It is a curious paradox that the greatest gifts of man, the unique faculties of conceptual thought and verbal speech which have raised him to a level high above all other creatures and given him mastery over the globe, are not altogether blessings, or at least are blessings that have to be paid for very dearly indeed. All the great dangers threatening humanity with extinction are direct consequences of conceptual thought and verbal speech. They drove man out of the paradise in which he could follow his instincts with impunity and do or not do whatever he pleased.' Konrad Lorenz, *On Aggression*, 204.

new body's capacity to extend itself, to create new organs (instruments or tools) combined with an unusual perpetuation of infancy behaviour into adult life (so that humans continue throughout life to explore their world in play) resulted in the development of symbolic behaviour and hence of language. Gradually there grew up the precarious structure of the new kind of animal grouping, a group held together not by the firm and sure bonds of instinct but by the much more fragile but immensely more effective links of a shared culture. An animal society emerges that is constituted by personal relationship, by communication which demands an openness, a capacity for self-giving. Human society is in the end constituted by love.

The problem for the linguistic animal is that the linguistic social community, the group within which there can be established relationships of communication, is never co-extensive with the genetic community. Men are not able to communicate with each other simply in virtue of being of one species, but only if they belong to one particular group. It was no doubt inevitable that this should be so. Systems of conventional signs would be developed in very local communities, and it is not at all surprising that communication should be achieved in one group at the expense of others, so that linguistic communities are not merely separate from each other but mutually hostile. One hypothesis about the development of the linguistic animal represents man as primarily a killer, emerging first of all as a hunting pack, a form of animal grouping in which a very intense relationship within the group is combined with ferocity towards everything outside. Amongst men, since their groups are constituted largely by conventional signs and not by genetically determined factors, a different group will have a different language and hence be seen as alien. Something parallel to this is to be found amongst certain kinds of rat which form communities distinguished from each other by smell. They are one of the few species which share the human characteristics of murder and warfare. With the rats, however, at least the smell is reliable. Unless an experimenter cruelly uses a deodorant, a rat within its own community is perfectly safe. Language is a much chancier thing. A smell is just a smell and stays that way, but a language has a history and is constantly developing. Those who at one time shared your language and other customs may drift away so that separate, competing and finally hostile groups are formed.

Because of this the development of communication, the growth of human culture, is not a simple or a single story. It consists, in fact, of a series of attempts to establish a stable human community, a stable area of communication, all of which attempts have ended in failure. As the very profound 'fall' story in Genesis 11 shows us, the attempt to build the city and the tower, to create a human identity, ('make a name for ourselves lest we be scattered abroad upon the face of the whole earth') collapses in failure of communication. Similarly Luke in his story of Pentecost sees a symbol of the beginning of the kingdom in the restoration of communication between men of different languages. As communication becomes more intense it becomes more isolated. Consider the university, an institution wholly devoted to the exploration of new modes of communication; just because of this preoccupation it inevitably alienates itself from the total social community and in so doing finally trivialises itself. We have seen the same thing happening with the christian churches. Beginning as a group of people concerned in a particular way with the world, they slip into being a group concerned about this particular kind of concern; they become interested in christianity instead of being interested in the world. The result has always been a trivialised church, one that seems to have little relevance to the society it is supposed to transform. The periodical reforms of the church have always been concerned to remedy this situation. The story of mankind is thus a story of failures and yet there is undoubtedly progress. Perhaps, however, it is like the progress of an unsuccessful gambler who doubles his stake every time he loses. As our attempts at civilisation get more sophisticated and more extensive the cost of failure rises. The collapse of any earlier culture was always a setback for mankind; the bomb suggests that the collapse of the American culture may be the end of the whole thing.

The bible presents us with the idea that man is *summoned*, that he is called to a destiny, that, in fact, his history has a meaning. When the story of mankind is finished it will be seen to have had a pattern; what now seems arbitrary and absurd will be seen by hindsight to have had a part to play in a significant whole. In other words mankind will achieve an identity. I suggested earlier that to have an identity, to answer the question 'who am I?' is to be able to write an autobiography, to provide an interpretation of one's past life. Similarly for a nation to have an identity is for it to be able to write its history. Now the biblical view of man is that he *will be able* to write a history of mankind. The bible itself is not such a history; it is the story of a people whose history is a sacrament of the history of mankind. (I shall explain later what I mean by 'sacrament' here.) To confuse the sacred history as recounted in the bible with the history we are finally to write when mankind has achieved its identity would be like confusing the christian community with the kingdom of God. The biblical view, then, is that men are called to become mankind, that in Christ we are to be able to create mankind.

> In this way we are all to come to unity in our faith and in our knowledge of the Son of God, until we become the perfect Man, fully mature with the fullness of Christ himself. [Eph 4:13]

However fragmented the human race may be at the moment—and this fragmentation which amounts to a deafness to the summons of God is seen as sin—it is moving towards a unity, a point of view from which its history will be intelligible. Such a movement can only take place through what I have earlier called revolutionary change; not by mere progress along the established lines, but by radical transformation of the lines themselves.

Since men can in fact only find their present partial identities in smaller mutually hostile groups, the summons to an identity for mankind implies a constant call to novelty, to creative advance. I mean that if I see myself as fundamentally an Englishman, as the product of a history in which Congolese and Cambodians have no real part (and I am speaking of how I *really* see myself, not of what I would piously say if questioned) then the call to identify myself as a member of the total community of mankind (a community that does not yet even exist) is a call to me to transcend my present image of myself. It means being prepared to give up the security of my present self to venture into a larger context. It means a constant criticism of the identity that is offered to me by my current language and other media of communication.

I think we may see the worship of the gods of the nations in the Old Testament as representing a settling for a partial local identity. To worship the local gods meant seeing oneself as essentially belonging to this tribe, this place, this time. The gods were closely tied to the soil of a particular region, to the fixed rhythms of nature, to the structures of a particular society. The call away from this to the worship of the non-god Yahweh meant a radical dissatisfaction with any such establishment.

It may be worth while at this point to take a look at the revelation of Yahweh on Mount Sinai, and in particular at the ten commandments which are, as I have suggested earlier, an account of the God of Israel.

> I am Yahweh your God who brought you out of the land of Egypt, out of the house of slavery. You shall have no gods except me. [Ex 20]

Yahweh announces himself first of all as the God of freedom, the one who summons Israel out of slavery. His first characteristic is to be a liberating God. Now it must seem a strange thing that the first thing the God of freedom should do is to lay commands and restrictions on his people—and such absolute and uncompromising commands. You might expect the God of freedom to leave men free to make their own decisions and run their own lives. Freedom, we might expect, would consist in people doing what they liked. As a matter of theory this is no doubt true but, as we have seen, there are various complications attending the notion of 'doing what you want'. As a matter of history one of the peculiar things about man is that when he is left to do exactly what he likes he straight away looks around for someone to enslave himself to, and if he cannot find a master nearby he will invent one. The Hebrew discovery of God (or God's revelation of himself to them) begins in their recognition that man historically is a slave, and enslaved by his own preference. The true God reveals himself as he who summons man out of this degradation that he clings to, who summons him to the painful business of being free.

The history of all revolutions documents the extreme reluctance that all peoples have to be liberated. After the event we may claim that 'in every generation the Irish people have asserted their right to national freedom and sovereignty: six times during the past three hundred years they have asserted it in arms,'[1] but a more exact look at the events indicates that these revolts were invariably the work of a small minority and that nearly all the time nearly all the people were either not particularly interested in freedom or actively opposed to it. (We may remember the actual attitude of the people of Dublin to the signatories of the *Proclamation* immediately after the failure of the rising.) We may, indeed, rightly assert after the event that the minority of

[1] *Proclamation of the Irish Republic*, Easter 1916.

active revolutionaries did in fact speak for the deepest desires of the apparently indifferent majority, but most people could not be aware of this at the time. The Hebrews were probably the only people in the world who even in their official propaganda about their own revolution took an entirely honest and realistic view of the events. Exodus describes in some detail the immense reluctance of the people to be liberated; they had to be practically dragged out of Egypt by the hand of Yahweh. We may well imagine how the Egyptians complained of the terrorist methods of Moses and his fellow agitators to intimidate a people who really only wanted to be left alone to serve their masters. Now such reluctance to be liberated may in many cases be due to a well-founded scepticism about the reality of the freedom offered, but beneath it all is man's constant fear of freedom, of departing from the familiar limits of his prison. The Hebrews at any rate saw their revolution as a revelation from God; they saw reluctance to take part as deafness to the summons of the God of freedom; for them the paradigm case of sin was settling for the comfort of slavery in Egypt.

Yahweh is the God of freedom and there are to be no other gods. 'The prohibition of "other gods" is the basic demand made of Israel'.[1] The important thing is not just to be religious, to worship something somehow. The important thing is to find, or be found by, the right God and to reject and struggle against the others. The worship of any other god is a form of slavery; to pay homage to the forces of nature, to the spirit of a particular place, to a nation or race or to anything that is too powerful for you to understand or control is to submit to slavery and degradation. The Old Testament religion begins by saying to such gods 'I do not believe and I will not serve'. The only true God is the God of freedom. The other gods make you feel at home in a place, they have to do with the quiet cycle of the seasons, with the familiar mountains and the country you grew up in and love; with them you know where you are. But the harsh God of freedom calls you out of all this into a desert where all the old familiar landmarks are gone, where you cannot rely on the safe workings of nature, on springtime and harvest, where you must wander over the wilderness waiting for what God will bring. This God of freedom will allow you none of the

[1] Noth, 162. 'The unconditional exclusiveness of the recognition and worship of the God of Israel stands rightly as *the* most important point at the beginning of the series of divine commandments.'

comforts of religion. Not only does he tear you away from the old traditional shrines and temples of your native place, but he will not even allow you to worship *him* in the old way. You are forbidden to make an image of him by which you might wield numinous power, you are forbidden to invoke his name in magical rites. You must deny the other gods and you must not treat Yahweh as a god, as a power you could use against your enemies or to help you to succeed in life. Yahweh is not a god, there are no gods, they are all delusions and slavery. You are not to try to comprehend God within the conventions and symbols of your time and place; you are to have no image of God because the only image of God is man.

We have already seen in chapter 2 that the command to observe the sabbath is not a regulation about the worship of Yahweh. The sabbath is not a day for going to the temple, for sacrifice or special prayers. Primarily 'you shall do no work on that day'. This commandment is aimed against the idolatry of work. Just as all idols are 'the work of men's hands' so this work may always become an idol, a means of alienation. As Karl Marx pointed out, in the class-structured society:

The more the worker expends himself in work,

> the more powerful becomes the world of objects which he creates in face of himself, and the poorer he himself becomes in his inner life, the less he belongs to himself.[1]

And Marx perceptively adds 'it is just the same as in religion'. For the 'religion' that Marx knew of was precisely the idolatry condemned in Exodus.

The sabbath is there to stop you being absorbed in the success story, to prevent you being enslaved to productivity and profit. This command is followed by a very similar one, 'honour your father and mother so that you may have long life . . .' This is not a commandment for children; it has nothing to do with obeying lawful authority. It has to do with the old and useless. To respect people just because they are images of the God of freedom even though they are no longer any 'use' is a test of the worship of Yahweh alone. The idolatrous society will characteristically neglect and try to forget the aged.

The rest of the ten commandments are a kind of definition of the idolatrous society out of which we are called by Yahweh. You shall not kill: the idolatrous society is the society of violence. The word used here is not quite the same as the English word 'kill'. Hebrew has special words which are normally used for killing

[1] *Selected Writings in Sociology*, 178.

in battle and for putting a man to death. It does not seem to be these that are in question here. Nor, however, can we translate it by the word 'murder' for the word is also used to cover accidental killing. The commandment, then, says not merely that you must not actually murder but that you must *care* that people get killed. You must not be indifferent to blood. You must not carry on the old traditional respectable life while in the back streets the police are shooting down the poor. You must not sit absorbed in the worship of your gods while throughout the world people are being killed by the horrible pain of hunger and the diseases that go with it, or by the 'accidental' deaths that go with slum life. (A couple of years ago children in the Chicago Negro ghetto were being killed or blinded by the cheap but poisonous lead paint that the slum landlords had used; others were attacked by rats that bred in the uncollected rubbish in the streets. The commandment is directed against this kind of violence and the indifference that causes it.) You shall not commit adultery; you must respect the family life of weaker men and not believe that because you have the gods on your side, your wealth, your good looks, your attractiveness, you are entitled to ignore the humanity of others.

You shall not steal. Certainly the most misunderstood of all the commandments. It has nothing to do with property and its so-called rights. What it refers to is stealing men.[1] Taking away their freedom to enslave them. It is a curious irony that in the name of this commandment we have built up a whole theory of the sacredness of possessions, of objects, a theory that has led to the wholesale enslavement of men—the very thing the commandment in fact denounces. The slavery of men is, together with violence, the great characteristic of the idolatrous society. And so the commandments go on to complete the picture of the society that worships the work of men's hands, where justice is perverted ('you shall not bear false witness') and the weak are the victims of rapacity and covetousness.

The idolatrous society thus presents two faces; on the one hand it is a religious society with great respect for the traditional ways; it will be a society in which patriotism is highly valued and in which there is much concern for the country's 'heritage'. On the other hand it will also be a society of institutionalised violence in

[1] 'It is today regarded as certain that the prohibition of stealing referred originally to the kidnapping of a free person.' Gerhard von Rad, *Deuteronomy*, London 1966, 59. cf Noth, 165–166.

which brutality and injustice is either hidden or given a mask of legality. It is important to see that any society may become idolatrous in this way, that in fact every society betrays a built-in tendency to such a worship of the work of man's hands. In any society men are liable to find their identity simply in what they themselves have achieved; the rejection of this is the beginning of the discovery of Yahweh.

Yahweh constantly calls man to grow up yet more; to leave behind the established and the secure, first the security of the local nature gods, but then even the security of the Hebrew religious system itself:

> Yet here you are, trusting in delusive words, to no purpose. Steal, would you, murder, commit adultery, perjure yourselves, burn incense to Baal, follow alien gods that you do not know?—and then come presenting yourselves in this Temple that bears my name, saying 'now we are safe'—safe to go on committing all these abominations. Do you take this Temple that bears my name for a robbers' den? I, at any rate, am not blind—It is Yahweh who speaks. (Jer 7:8–11)

The response to this God who summons man into the future is always one of faith, of venturing forward into an area of which we have no maps.

The process is the familiar one of growing up. You cannot grow up unless you are prepared to leave behind the securities of childhood. On the other hand you cannot grow up without a trust in the adult world, without a different kind of security resting not on a framework of 'what is done and what is not done' but on a personal relationship with adults. With the confidence that comes from being loved, a child becomes able to jettison the security of a system and an order that is no longer adequate to him. When Jesus refers to 'your Father' I think it is this that he has in mind. He is not in the first place, it seems to me, thinking of the father as progenitor, as the source of being, he is rather thinking of the relationship between the father and the growing child—where the father is, in a new sense, a source of existence. Without faith in his father the child will not be able to develop and become himself. The father is the figure who challenges us to set aside childish things and grow up. To put it another way, a communication with the adult world is established through the father, and this enables the child to criticise the styles of communication that belong to his childhood; it enables him to transcend himself. His communication with the father does not give him a clear and unambiguous identity, he sees but as in a glass darkly, but it does help him to criticise the picture of himself that he has hitherto had. It is only when the growing up is completed that he achieves his new identity as an adult with his father. Now in a somewhat similar way the communication with Yahweh enables man to criticise his present world, his present society, in terms of a future development which he can for the moment only dimly understand.

So long as the communication from Yahweh is seen simply as a summons, as a command to grow up, it serves to accentuate man's hopeless position. It helps him to criticise his world, his merely particularised local existence, but it does not, by itself, help him to transcend it. In St Paul's view, the law seen simply as an account of the idolatrous society becomes itself a kind of slavery, but we have to see the law as belonging to a larger context, the context of Yahweh's *promise*. To see the giving of the law as having its place in the promise of Yahweh is to see it as a partial communication by Yahweh of himself to men. This promise, this self-giving of Yahweh, is only fully realised in Jesus of Nazareth.

# 5
# The word as love

The centre of the gospel is that in Jesus Yahweh communicates himself wholly to us. There are two fundamental things to be said about Jesus: one is that he is the word of Yahweh, the self-communication of God, the other that he is the meaning of human history. It would be to betray a tritheistic rather than a trinitarian view to imagine that the New Testament records the coming of the Son instead of the coming of the Father. In Jesus we have the visitation of Yahweh of which the prophets spoke. The word of God is the way in which the Father sees himself, his realisation of himself; the incarnation means that this divine self-realisation is shared with us. We are able to enter into the language, and hence the life, of the Father. This self-giving of the Father is the meaning of human history because what man is meant for, what he is summoned to, is to share the life of the Father—on the analogy of a child growing up to share the life of his parents. Jesus, then, the communication of the Father, is mankind come to its meaning; it is because of him that mankind makes sense. These are dark sayings; let me try to illuminate them.

First of all what do we not mean. Imagine a manufacturer of doorknobs who keeps making mistakes so that his doorknobs come out all wrong. Gradually he perfects his technique and finally comes up with the perfect doorknob. He might say, 'That is what I have been trying to do all this time. This perfect doorknob gives meaning and sense to all those long dark days of effort. This is what it was all for'. Now we are not saying simply that after a long series of defective men we finally come to the perfect man, Jesus, who thus makes the whole thing seem worthwhile. The essential difference is that each doorknob is a separate thing, it exists by itself and does not depend for its existence on its relationship to other doorknobs. The manufacture of doorknobs is just the making of one example after another, each one an isolated entity, whereas the making of men is the making of mankind; a man exists in his relationship to others. The perfect man, then, the being that man was meant to be, cannot be just an individual example of the human race, his perfection will consist in his setting up a new kind of relationship to the rest of mankind.

To be a man is to be a centre of society, it is to be in communication with other men (and also, as we have seen, in a sense, in communication with things—at least in the unilateral sense of conferring significance on them, constituting them a world). The imperfect man is the centre of a limited society, his capacity for communication is exhausted by this society and supported by a hostility to others. I mean that each of us finds himself, finds his identity, in the centre of our group of friends or fellow-countrymen or whatever. A social grouping is constituted by the overlapping social worlds of its members. Because they overlap there is a common world. This world is held together mainly by the common ties between its members but there is also the important external factor of exclusiveness. It is held together not only by love but also by fear, one of its bonds is a common hostility to what is alien. This is quite a common feature of other animal societies and it is part of the heritage we have somehow to transcend if we are to achieve real human unity.

The claim that Jesus is perfectly human is the claim that his social world is co-extensive with humanity, that he is open to all men and moreover open to all that is in man. It is not just that he would like to be or that he proposes this as an ideal (this would be true of any liberal philosopher) but that he actually is; the communication he offers is unmixed with domination or exclusiveness. So the coming of Jesus would not be just the coming of an individual specimen of the excellent or virtuous man, a figure whom we might try to imitate, but the coming of a new humanity, a new kind of community amongst men. For this reason we can compare the coming of Jesus to the coming of a new language; and indeed, John does this: Jesus is the word, the language of God which comes to be a language for man.

Jesus is the future destiny of mankind (to which we are summoned by the Father) trying to be present amongst men in our present age. He offers a new way in which men can be together, a new way in which they can be free to be themselves, the way of total self-giving, and he offers this in amongst the various makeshift ways in which men have tried to build community. Specifically he offers it amongst the men of a late Hebrew culture who have become part of the Roman colonial empire. I must make this word 'offer' clear. Jesus is not offering a blueprint for a new kind of society, an ideal which men may or may not choose to realise, he is offering *himself* as the centre of this new society, as the source of a new kind of personal relationship. He provides a new mode of communication and one which you can only recognise by participating in it. If you look at it from outside it does not even look like a possible blueprint. If, still thinking in terms of the already constituted society, you examine what Jesus seems to be advocating, it merely looks destructive. 'Offer the wicked man no resistance . . . Give to anyone who asks . . . Do not worry about tomorrow, tomorrow will take care of itself . . .' The objection to all this is not that it would be difficult to fulfil but that human society would collapse if we took it literally—we have, have we not, to be realistic about these things. But Matthew ends this section of his gospel with 'his teaching made a deep impression on the people because he taught them with authority, and not like their own scribes'. He was offering himself, in fact, as the *author* of this kind of communication amongst men. He was not, like the scribes, commenting on a law, but establishing a new kind of community. But seen from outside, seen as a scribe might see it, his teaching looks destructive; and this, of course, is how it looked to the religious leaders of his time—they took him for a heretic—and to the colonial government and their puppet regime—they found him a political nuisance, a trouble-maker.

When the divine future of mankind tries to be present to the world as men have painfully constructed it, the consequence is hardly in doubt. he is rejected. This is the event I compared to the unleashing of total nuclear war. A perfectly ordinary group of harassed ecclesiastics, politicians and soldiers happened to have the fate of the world in their hands. Of course once it has happened, looking back you can see that the world was leading up to this—during the four minute warning one might just have time for a hasty re-interpretation of history in terms of movement towards the bomb.[1]

The crucifixion of Christ is the occasion of just such a re-interpretation of human history. In the light of this final rejection we can see that all failures of communication take their sense from this refusal; they are not just failures, they are part of a pattern of *sin*. For this is what sin first

[1] Though there is, of course, a sense in which such things are 'unnecessary'. cf de Selby, *Layman's Atlas* Cop 3, 93.

of all means for a christian. Anyone can see that the linguistic animal is imperfect, that its whole future is in danger, not from outside but from self-destruction. The christian point is that this amounts to a historical rejection of an offer of divinity, a rejection of transcendence, a rejection by mankind of its own meaning, centred on the rejection of Jesus. 'The sin of the world came to a climax in the crucifixion of Christ. This is the Fall in the most radical sense: the killing of the uniquely Good, the expulsion of God.'[1]

After the crucifixion, to interpret the defect of the world as sin, to interpret it, that is, as involving the rejection of the Father's self-giving, is the same as to say that given the sin of the world, the crucifixion was bound to happen. It is to say that this is the kind of world we have, a crucifying world, a world doomed to reject its own meaning. In so far as a man calls men to a deeper kind of humanity, in so far as he offers them, not just in theory but in practice, a more human mode of communication, he will be

[1] *A New Catechism*, London 1967, 267. For a more detailed discussion of this question see Timothy McDermott OP 'Original Sin', *New Blackfriars* (Jan and Feb, 1968). The January issue also contains a critical account by Cornelius Ernst OP of the doctrine of sin presented in *A New Catechism.*

rejected by mankind. The openness of love becomes the vulnerability of the victim. If you love enough you will in the long run be killed. I do not say that the two things are the same: to be a victim is a sign of love, but only a sign; a man may seek the status of victim as a substitute for loving—I can offer my body to be burned and not have charity. Jesus does not seek victimisation; the Son of God did not come to us in order to be crucified, but since he comes to be a totally loving, totally human human being, it was inevitable that he would be crucified. At least we can see this now by hindsight. What he came to do was to bring a new life, a new form of human communication out of this crucifying world. His resurrection means that this is possible.

The resurrection of Christ means that death is not just a matter of destruction, the end of life, but can be a revolution; the beginning of a new and unpredictable life. All revolution means a radical change in the structures within which we have our existence, all revolution produces a new kind of man; resurrection is the revolution through death, the radical change of those structures within which we exist at all. I mean that a man can survive other revolutions; there are structures, the structures of the body, which remain untouched by the most radical changes in his other media of communication. Resurrection means that because of his link with the Father in Christ a man can suffer the destruction even of those basic structures, the ones that constitute his body, and rediscover his identity on the far side of death. Because the current world is crucifying, Christ-rejecting, even in its bodily structure, mankind can only achieve its destiny, its unity in love, through a revolution that goes as deep as this, through the revolution of death. The new world comes only through the death of this world. Thus every revolution which deals with structures less ultimate than this is an image of, and a preparation for, the resurrection of the dead. The Cuban or Vietnamese revolution is a *type* of the resurrection in the sense that we speak of Old Testament events as types of Christ. In a sense every revolution draws upon powers that are not catered for in the preceding society, powers which therefore seem to be invisible because they transcend the terms of that society: 'we are not just peasants, we are men, though you have forgotten it'. The power and the spirit of every revolution thus comes from 'outside' the society that is overthrown. The power and the spirit of the ultimate revolution, the resurrection, comes from 'outside' man altogether. For the christian, this is what divinity is: God is he who raised Jesus from the dead.

> If the Spirit of him who raised Jesus from the dead dwells in you, he who raised Christ Jesus from the dead will give life to your mortal bodies also through his Spirit which dwells in you. [Rm 8:11 (RSV)]

The transcendence of God is defined in terms of the ultimate revolution, it has nothing to do with whether we like to speak of God as 'up there' or 'in here'. The quarrel of the christian with the marxist about God is not a matter of the validity of the 'five ways', nor is it a matter of whether a man should have the right to worship whatever way he likes in his spare time; it concerns the nature of revolution and the interpretation of Jesus. If the marxist is right and there is no God who raised Jesus from the dead then the christian pre-occupation with death as the ultimate revolutionary act is a diversion from the real demands of history; if the christian is right then the marxist is dealing with revolution only at a relatively superficial level, he has not touched the ultimate alienation involved in death itself, and for this reason his revolution will betray itself; the liberation will erect a new idol. Not that the christian church is in any position to cast the first stone at people who betray their own revolutionary purpose.

The new world, then, comes about through the death of this world. My own personal choice is whether to belong to this world, to find my identity and the meaning of my life in terms of the structures that constitute this world, or whether to accept its death and seek my identity in terms of a world to come. When I speak of 'this world' and contrast it with a 'world to come' beyond death, I am not thinking of a shadow world that exists alongside this material world inhabited by dead people instead of living ones. I am not, in fact, thinking of what has come to be meant by 'heaven'. I am thinking of the future of this world; not, however, its future in an evolutionary or teilhardian sense, but in a revolutionary sense—a future which will be *of* this world, continuous with this world, in a way that will only be clear after the revolution has occurred. For this reason the question whether the kingdom of God will come on earth is an ambiguous one: if it means will the kingdom come somewhere *else*, the answer is 'no'; if it means will the kingdom come within the recognisable structures of this world, within structures that would develop predictably from this world, then the answer must also be 'no'.

The idea that to belong to Christ, to have your identity in terms of the world centred on him, is to belong to the world of the future and not simply to this world, this idea, known as the doctrine of the resurrection of the dead, ought not to be confused with belief in the immortality of the soul. The first is a central christian doctrine, the second a secondary matter which does not even find mention in the early creeds. I think that a Roman catholic is probably committed to the immortality of the soul, mainly because of the practice of praying to saints and praying for the dead; but in any case it is one thing to believe this and quite another to believe that those who 'sleep in Christ' will rise again from the dead in the future. Before leaving this topic there are two more points that are perhaps worth making. One is that the sketch I have given makes no mention of the resurrection of those who reject Christ that seems to be referred to in John 5:29. St Paul too, in his epistles, makes no mention of this; for him resurrection is always a sharing in the resurrection of Christ.[1] The other point is that we must beware of confusing resurrection with resuscitation. The return to life of, say, Lazarus, or for that matter the manifestations of Jesus himself after the resurrection are merely

[1] But see Acts 24:15.

symbols of the new risen life.[1] Resurrection is much more catastrophic than this; it is a revolution, not merely a return to the *status quo ante*. Nor, however, if we are to maintain a revolutionary continuity between the risen life and previous existence, can we separate off the resurrection of Christ from the empty tomb. It was in his body that he died and was transformed.[2]

[1] 'When we look at the risen Christ, taking into consideration the experience the Apostles had with him, we may also get some idea of what the perfected condition of the body is like in which the created spirit achieves itself. Only in doing this we must not forget that what the Apostles, being themselves as yet unachieved, were able to experience of this consummation, is a somewhat broken translated experience, and that even then it still remains obscure how the perfection appears to the perfected.' Karl Rahner, 'The Resurrection of the Body', *Theological Investigations* II, London 1963, 214.

[2] 'Sans doute, ce corps qui est ressuscité en Jésus, et qui ressuscitera en nous, est-il un corps spiritualisé, devenu céleste, mais c'est bien le même corps qui, après avoir été enseveli dans la corruption, renaît d'une vie nouvelle et incorruptible, le corps "psychique" devenu corps "pneumatique".

Toute la doctrine paulinienne s'oriente sur cette Résurrection corporelle du Christ comme sur un de ses points cardinaux. En le Christ, et en lui seul pour le moment, s'est déjà opéré le renouveau cosmique qui doit charactériser l'ère eschatologique. Le corps ressuscité de Jésus est la cellule première du Cosmos nouveau. En lui l'Esprit a déjà

Jesus failed to affect human history from within, he failed to bring it to a head, he was crucified instead. If it were not that christianity kept his memory alive, the life and death of Jesus would have passed almost unnoticed and soon have been forgotten. It did not have the historical importance of, say, the murder of Julius Caesar or Patrice Lumumba. Neither the world as a whole nor even the Roman empire in the Middle East seemed to be in any way affected. We might say that if Jesus had not been

---

pris possession de la matière, comme il doit le faire de toute la Création, après la Parousie, quand le Christ "récapitulera" définitivement toutes choses. Tant que l'ère présente se continue, les corps des autres hommes ne participent pas encore à ce triomphe; ils restent soumis à la loi de la mort et de la corruption. Cependant ceux de ses fidèles sont déjà unis au sien par l'union mystique du Baptême et de l'Eucharistie; avec lui ils sont morts et ressuscités. Ce qui est pour lui un état physique et définitif est pour eux un état mystique et qui attend son achèvement, mais qui n'en est pas moins réel. C'est sur ces bases très concrètes que se construisent la morale et la mystique si réalistes de S. Paul. Si les corps des chrétiens sont dès maintenant à ses yeux les "temples de l'Esprit Saint", s'ils sont sanctifiés et purifiés jusque dans leurs passions physiques, c'est parce qu'ils sont rattachés par le moyen des sacrements au Corps glorifié de leur Maître. Ils sont ses membres et se préparent à le rejoindre dans son existence céleste par leur propre résurrection, qui surviendra lors de sa Parousie.' P. Benoit OP, 'l'Ascension', *Revue Biblique* LVI (1949), 181–182.

rejected this would not have been the case; the new kind of human community—the kingdom of God—would have been established, history would have come to a head or, if you like, pre-history would have come to an end. We know, however, at least by hindsight, that Jesus was bound to be rejected. Human history was such, was so determined by sin, that it could not accommodate the kind of human relationships that Jesus proposed.

Because Jesus failed he did not (like, say, Thomas Jefferson) lay the foundations of a new kind of society. He did not represent something to which men could look back and from which they could go forward. Because of his resurrection, because he was able to achieve his mission through failure, he is relevant to men not as past but as future. Ordinarily we would say that the past like the present exists, whereas the future does not. The past, like the present, has a real effect upon us, and like the present it determines the truth of propositions. The future, on the other hand, we should ordinarily say, does not exist and cannot have any effect upon us. In the risen Christ, however, the future exists and influences the present in a way comparable to the way the past does. Jesus Christ is himself the medium in which men will in the future communicate, he is the body in which we shall all be interrelated members, '*la cellule première du cosmos nouveau*,' he is the language in which we shall express ourselves to each other in accordance with the promise and summons of the Father. Now this language, this medium of expression, this body which belongs to the future is made really present for us in the church.

There are many groups whose purpose is to ensure that something of the *past* is made real for the present, whether it be the Glorious Revolution or the taking of the Bastille or the Smashing of the Van; this indeed is the purpose of any group that seeks to preserve the historical identity of a people. Such remembrance is a very large part of the business of education—to recognise and realise our past is to discover ourselves. Now the business of the church is to 'remember' the future. Not merely to remember that there is to be a future, but mysteriously to make the future really present. This is uniquely possible in the case of Christ because of his resurrection. He was expelled from the course of history by his rejection, his crucifixion, but his resurrection means that he remains present to history though in a non-historical way. The articulation of this presence is the church: I mean that the church makes the presence of

Christ articulate as a language, as an interpretation of the world, as a means of communication.

This is rather an important point. There are christians who hold that the resurrection of Christ means that, although he died, he still lives on in the faith of his followers—a faith expressed by word and sacrament in the church. The basic catholic objection to this is that it makes of the resurrection a religious event, one that makes a difference primarily to what happens in the church; whereas for the catholic tradition the resurrection is a cosmic event, it means that Christ is present to the whole world whether believers or not. The resurrection meant not just that a church was founded, it meant that the world was different: the church exists to articulate this difference, to show the world to itself.[1] We say that the church in the proclamation of the gospel, and in particular in the sacraments, makes Christ, our future, really present but not

[1] 'The truth is that only in the mystery of the incarnate Word does the mystery of man take on light. For Adam, the first man, was a figure of him who was to come, Christ the Lord. Christ, the final Adam, by the revelation of the mystery of the Father and his love, fully reveals man to man himself and makes his supreme calling clear' *Gaudium et Spes* 22, *Documents of Vatican* II, ed W. M. Abbot, SJ, London 1966.

as though he were previously absent; the difference lies in the mode in which he is present.

The sacramental life is the creative interpretation of the world in terms of the presence to it of Christ, its future. Let me explain that. A political cartoonist provides an interpretation of his victim; his purpose is to articulate or draw attention to what he regards as the fundamental meaning of his subject's political policy. Now the politician may in fact be helped by the cartoonist to understand his own policies more clearly. He may begin to see himself in terms of the cartoon. In a sense we are constantly making cartoons of ourselves; we have an image of ourselves, a simplified image which brings out what we regard as our essential character, an image in terms of which we interpret our autobiography. Such an image is a *realisation* of ourselves in two possible senses of the word: it is both a recognition of who and what we are and also a making real of who and what we are. We can speak of it as a *creative* interpretation of the self. Now, of course, a cartoon is not a very good example of what I mean because it remains at a deliberately superficial level but the point is that it can have this dual role of interpretation and creation. Let us take another example. I spoke earlier of the fact that revolutionaries are always a small minority in a population. They are usually an unpopular minority, apparently rejected by the masses, and yet after the revolution has succeeded it is not a distortion of history to see them as representative of the people. It is not a lie to dramatise the revolutionary history as though the people were enthusiastic about the movement. Very crudely, the reason for this is that for the majority of the people, especially in a pre-revolutionary and mystified society, their political views are not the expression of their real beliefs and desires. If you ask them to talk politics they will play a game which has little relevance to their actual lives. Now the revolutionary whom they would condemn because they see him as destructive and a nuisance in their political terms may in fact be the spokesman of their real concerns which are not allowed to impinge on what they regard as politics. It is only when the revolution has changed and demystified the meaning of the word 'politics' that we can see how the revolutionary or 'terrorist' was in fact the representative of his people. Until that time the revolution demands faith. The revolutionary is creatively interpreting the life of his people, he points to where it is going (even though most people cannot yet see themselves clearly enough to recognise this) and he helps to make it go there.

Now it is in somewhat this sense that the church, the 'sacrament of the unity of mankind'[1] is a continuing creative interpretation of human life; revealing and realising in her proclamation of the gospel (a great part of which is her sacramental life) the presence of the risen Christ to the world; revealing therefore and realising the revolutionary future of the world. The sacramental life as a whole, centring on the eucharist, is an articulation both of human life now in its real but only dimly discernible revolutionary depth and of the world to come. It is only by the utter openness implied in faith that the revelation of this depth and this future can be received.

It is because the sacramental life of the church is an entry into the deep meaning of human existence—an entry which is not merely a theoretical study but an actual encounter with the future reality that lies at the heart of human meaning—that it makes us able to take human

[1] 'Sacramentum seu signum et instrumentum intimae cum Deo unionis totiusque generis humani unitatis.' Second Vatican Council, *Lumen Gentium* 1.

behaviour seriously, to make moral decisions and judgements. The sacraments function in our moral life neither by giving us the extra will-power needed to keep in line with a moral code, nor by providing a pattern of life from which such a code might be theoretically deduced. They function more as does the experience of literature or drama: providing us with an insight, (but a uniquely authentic insight) into the nature and destiny of man, an insight which we may or may not—according to our intellectual capacities—be able to verbalise approximately in the form of principles.

Let me explain in the briefest possible way the kind of thing that I mean by speaking of the sacraments as an articulation of the deep meaning of human living. Baptism/confirmation, the entry through conversion into the christian movement, is the sacrament of birth. Not just because it is analogous to birth but in the sense that it is the sacramental expression of joining the human race; it brings out what it actually means to be born. Baptism is not the sacrament of membership of the church, it *is* membership of the church; it is the sacrament of membership of mankind. We speak of baptism as a re-generation or a re-birth but we should not be misled by that *re-*. Baptism is not a second birth that we have instead of the first; we are not discarding the first; still less are we adding something on top of it—a layer of grace-life on top of the natural life we received at birth. In this second birth we are discovering the implications of our first birth. Birth to be true to itself has to be re-birth. To be born is to be born into a revolutionary situation, it is to be born for the final revolution of death. If we are to join the human race it is not enough to be born into it, it is also necessary to die into it and this is what baptism proclaims. It is a symbolic death, a creative sign of our dying the revolutionary death of Christ, out of which comes the new community:

> When we were baptised in Christ Jesus we were baptised in his death; in other words, when we were baptised we went into the tomb with him and joined him in death, so that as Christ was raised from the dead by the Father's glory, we too might live a new life. [Rm 6:3]

To be baptised is, then, to share in the condemnation of Christ, to be marked out for death, a death which will be a rejection by the world because it is the culminating point of a subversion of the world. Baptism interprets our birth, our joining the human race, as meant for our incorporation into Christ. We are born men in order to belong to the condemned Christ who is thereby the risen Christ. Confirmation similarly sees membership of the human race as meant for incorporation into the risen Christ who is thereby the source of the Spirit.[1] Baptism and confirmation show us two sides of that complete conformity to the mystery of Christ's redemptive act which is martyrdom: on the one hand death; on the other witness to truth.

The eucharist, the centre of the sacramental language, displays the revolutionary character of social life. As the sacraments of initiation show the ultimate significance of being born a member of mankind, so the eucharist shows the significance of all eating and drinking together, all sharing of life, all community. To say grace at any meal, to eat giving thanks, is to proclaim that the unity in life represented by the common

[1] 'From the earliest times baptism was thought of in association with Christ's death and resurrection, confirmation in association with the mystery of Pentecost. . . . (Christian) initiation is something that is fully achieved only by incorporation into Christ both as Son of the Father and as co-principle of the Spirit. Both these trinitarian relations acquire an historical, saving significance in the man Jesus; in his service as Son of the Father and in his human establishment in power as sender of the Spirit.' E. Schillebeeckx OP, *Christ the Sacrament*, London 1963, 199 and 201.

meal is a gift from the Father, to recognise that we only come to true human unity in response to his summons and by his help. To say grace is to make of any meal a thanks (or, in Greek, a 'eucharist'). The sacrament we call *the* eucharist is a creative interpretation of all man's attempts to form a community of love symbolised in the common table. The eucharist proclaims that all such attempts point towards a true society of love which is only achieved through the sacrificial love of Christ. As baptism is birth marked by death, so the eucharist is the meal marked by death.

> Until the Lord comes, therefore, every time you eat this bread and drink this cup, you are proclaiming his death. (1 Cor 11:26)

Just as we have to die into the human race, so we have to die into each other, we cannot simply live into each other. The eucharist proclaims the revolutionary significance of all human efforts towards community. In the eucharist the future world is made present to us; we already belong to the future, hence the close connection made in the New Testament between the eucharist and resurrection:

> If you do not eat the flesh of the Son of Man and drink his blood, you will not have life in

> you. Anyone who does eat my flesh and drink my blood has eternal life, and I shall raise him up on the last day. [Jn 6:53]

To speak of the real presence to us of Christ, our future life, in the eucharistic meal, and to speak of our presence to our future life, is to present two aspects of the same truth.

This book is not intended to include a detailed account of the sacramental life, but it is not difficult to see how each sacrament marks the intersection of the world to come with this present world; or, as we say, the presence of the risen Christ. In marriage the sexual life is interpreted in terms of its direction towards the new world. Sex is only fully itself, as birth is only fully itself, as eating and drinking together is only fully itself, when it discovers its deep orientation towards the future destiny of man in Christ:

> For this reason a man shall leave his father and mother and be joined to his wife, and the two shall become one'. This is a great mystery, and I take it to mean Christ and the church. [Eph 5:31]

It is not merely that sexual union is an appropriate image of Christ's relationship with mankind, but that sexual union finds its ultimate meaning in the consummation of this relationship.

The sacrament of penance explores the deep significance of forgiveness and its bodily expression which is non-violence. We may see non-violence as a technique, in which case it has its part to play in the revolutionary process, or we may see it in its deep meaning, in which case it is the whole of the revolutionary's purpose. There are times when the institutionalised violence of an unjust society can only be contained by revolutionary violence, but this will not by itself achieve anything; of itself it is counter-revolutionary. Violence can only be creative in a context of non-violence, as a part of forgiveness. The power of men in Christ to forgive and thereby transform the world and bring about the new society: this is what we show forth in the sacrament of penance. As all meals take their meaning from the sacrificial meal of Christ, so all forgiveness and non-violence takes its meaning and power from the forgiveness of Christ made articulately present to us in the sacrament of penance.

Again, the sacrament of order is an exploration into the deep meaning of revolutionary leadership. The christian minister is meant to be neither the pillar of an established quasi-feudal order, as conservative christians are inclined to think, nor is he the democratic representative of a quasi-bourgeois society as the progressives seem to suggest; he is a revolutionary leader whose job is the subversion of the world through the preaching of the gospel. He exercises authority amongst his people but not as maintaining an established structure; he is the leader of his people in a movement towards a new community. He is representative of his people but not necessarily in the sense of being their elected spokesman; he may represent them in the way a revolutionary leader does, a way that is not obvious to them and only becomes clear when the revolution is achieved. I think it significant that, according to St John, the first thing Jesus says about the missionaries he commissions before his death is that the world will hate them.

> Father . . . I passed your word on to them, and the world hated them, because they belong to the world no more than I belong to the world . . . As you sent me into the world, I have sent them into the world, and for their sake I consecrate myself [*a reference to his sacrificial death*] so that they too may be consecrated in truth. [Jn 17:14]

Finally we might speak of the sacrament of anointing the sick as an exploration of the meaning of the bodily care men have for each other, and see its ultimate meaning in Christ's care for our bodies culminating in the resurrection itself.

These very brief notes are intended merely to sketch the way in which we might fill out the statement that the sacramental life of the church makes the presence of the risen Christ articulate as a revolutionary interpretation of the world, an interpretation of the world in terms of its future destiny.

Life in Christ, then, is a seeking into the meaning of human behaviour which involves a constant reaching out beyond the values of the world. Sin consists in ceasing to reach out, refusing to respond to the Father's summons, and settling for this present world. What makes it possible for us to reach out, to hear and respond to the summons, is that through the resurrection of Christ the future world is already with us as a disruptive force disturbing the order of the world. We are able to some extent to live into the mode of communication that belongs to the future world, the mode we call charity or the presence of the Spirit. Of course trying to live in the present world a life in accordance with the future is a dangerous business, as Jesus found out. The christian may expect to be crucified with him.

One of my reasons for discussing, even so

briefly, the sacramental life, was to indicate that the business of reaching into the future is not a merely individual affair, not simply a matter for individual effort. Those who share the sacramental language, those who share sacramentally in the language of the future, form a community or, better, a movement within the world. It is this movement as a whole that seeks the revolution, that seeks the bearing of the future on the present. The discoveries of the church about the moral life are the result of a communal exploration, an exploration that has been going on with many set-backs and side-trackings for centuries. The authority of the christian community in the matter of morals is the authority of such a tradition: 'this is what living the life of Christ has been discovered to imply.' The authority of the New Testament is a part, the essential, originating part, of this tradition.

We are here, however, immediately confronted with a difficulty. The christian moral outlook is essentially drawn from our contact with the future. It is based upon the virtue of hope. It transcends the present and is never wholly explicable in terms of the present because it is revolutionary. For this reason, as we have seen, the christian moral position will always in the end seem unreasonable to the contemporary world. This is a good kind of 'unreasonableness'. On the other hand, since the christian moral outlook is formulated in the course of a long historical tradition that stretches far back into the past, it may be out of tune with the present for a different and much less respectable reason. It may be out of tune simply because its formulations belong to the past. This is more or less inevitable because they are the work of the whole christian community, and in this community, as in any community that has lasted for two thousand years, the great majority of the members have been dead for some time. It is necessary, then, in any age, for the living christians to disentangle these two factors; to discover to what extent they stand askew to the world because they are a revolutionary movement based on the future, and to what extent they stand askew merely because of their ties with the past. In what way is their cussedness eschatological and in what way is it merely old-fashioned? To what extent, for example, is the christian non-conformity in the matter of sexual morals conditioned by seeing sex in the light of the sacrament of marriage and to what extent is it conditioned merely by out of date and irrelevant social mores? In every age, I suppose, there will be conservatives who cling to a formulation arrived at in an earlier time and are hence at odds with the present, and there will be liberals in reaction against such conservatism who will frequently be merely conforming to this world. Both of these seem to me to be distortions of christianity, but the genuine radical christian will always be accused by each side of belonging to the other. This is not in the least because he is a 'moderate', but because he is opposed to both sides, seeing both as basically conformist—the one conforming to a past, the other to a present world.

The christian reaches out beyond this world towards a future world of freedom, towards real communication between men and therefore full human life. Such freedom, he will maintain, can never be an achieved static condition; it is only possible in a dynamic reaching out towards the Father. Man becomes fully human only by transcending humanity in divinity. The freedom with which he is concerned must not be confused with the individual autonomy bestowed on us by the industrial society; a society in which the the field of obligation has been reduced to that of work. A man must do what he is told during his work time, but in his leisure (non-work) he is free to do, believe, worship, read, what he likes. It is only in so far as these activities touch on the work relationship that they are restricted. This autonomy represents a new kind of society by comparison with the feudal one it replaced. It is the bourgeois secular city; the society in which the 'city' takes no official notice of anything except secular work-relationships and professes indifference to how its citizens play or paint or love or pray or speak with each other.[1] All such 'sacred' activities are free. (I call them 'sacred' in so far as they transcend the profane world which is more or less strictly regulated by social utility.) In the secular city a man is very nearly completely collectivised during his work time and very nearly a completely autonomous individual for the rest of the time. 'The modern subjectivity in which we today experience ourselves as individual and personal human beings, is a result of the disburdening of social intercourse by reducing it to terms of practical affairs.'[2] Progress in the bourgeois society essentially consists in diminishing as far as possible, by such means as

[1] 'The society which is dominated by the modernity and progressiveness of this civilisation has the peculiar characteristic of considering itself to be neutral towards matters of religion and questions of value and consequently emancipating itself from the control of history and tradition, whereby it also withdraws itself from the influence of religions and religious bodies.' Jürgen Moltmann, *Theology of Hope*, London 1967, 305.

[2] Moltmann, 309.

automation, the proportion of a man's life that is spent in the slavery of work. This liberal society is not yet a society of freedom in the christian sense. Freedom fundamentally means being able to give oneself and thereby realise oneself; a free society is a set of media in which people are able to be open to each other, to love each other without fear. The liberal society protects certain 'leisure' areas—the arts, religion, academic life—from interference and hence from fear, at the cost of separating them off from the other media of communication in the society, the areas, for example, of production and of government. In this society culture tends to become a private game which, because it is 'free', is free from relevance, and because it is irrelevant is not worth controlling. Philosophers, scientists, novelists and theologians need feel no responsibility towards the community in what they say because nobody takes them seriously. From time to time, of course, this programme breaks down and the liberal society becomes subject to fits of illiberalism.

The christian, as it seems to me, is not concerned to extend the areas of an autonomy which in the end means irresponsibility, but to transform media of domination into media of communication, media of self-assertion into media of self-expression. He is aware that this will never be finally achieved without a transfiguration of man, a radical revolution that reaches down to the depths of our bodily life and which therefore means death and resurrection. He is not, however, solely concerned with this ultimate revolution. His business is the continuing transformation of the world that leads up to this final parousia. The phrase 'leads up to' suggests a question which is commonly asked but which I think to be based on a misapprehension. We ask sometimes: should we regard the 'second coming', the resurrection, 'judgement day', the parousia, as the culmination of the work of christians in the world gradually leading up to this fulfilment; or should we think of it as something quite unexpected, as coming like a thief in the night, bursting in upon us and sweeping aside all the 'preparations' we have made. There can be little doubt that if the question is put that way, the second alternative is the one that finds most support in the New Testament. The difficulty that christians today find with this is that it suggests that any 'preparations' for the coming of Christ are an irrelevance; it suggests that christians have really no political role in the world, it is useless for them to try to transform society, they ought instead to retire into themselves and cultivate their inner lives. Eschatology ceases to be a *perspective* in the sense of a direction in history. The question is, however, misplaced. The assumption behind it is that we ought to choose between gradual progress, a steady ascent towards the last day, and a catastrophic break in history. The question, in fact, ignores the possibility of revolutionary advance. The parousia, I would want to say, does indeed come as the culmination of our efforts to transform the world, but it comes as the last of a series of revolutions, not as the final term of evolution. The second coming is indeed unexpected, sweeping aside what has gone before, but this is the very characteristic of revolutionary advance. Once we have grasped the idea of revolutionary change we can see how something can be quite new and unexpected and yet part of a continuity—a new kind of continuity which is only evident after the event.[1] It is in

[1] 'Therefore, while we are warned that it profits a man nothing if he gain the whole world and lose himself, the expectation of a new earth must not weaken but rather stimulate our concern for cultivating this one. For here grows the body of a new human family, a body which even now is able to give some kind of foreshadowing of the new age. Earthly progress must be carefully distinguished from the growth of Christ's kingdom. Nevertheless to the extent that the former can contribute to the better ordering of

this way that death is continuous with life. We see a man (or perhaps more commonly a woman) who seems to grow wiser and more deeply loving throughout her life, she seems to become more and more a living presence, a source of life to those around her, and then perhaps quite suddenly she dies. The first thought is of the absurdity of death; the contradiction between this accidental destruction and all the positive value that has gone before. But if, as the christian does, we see death as the final sacrifice, the final revolution, we find that death imposes its new perspective on the life that went before, we realise that exactly what we meant by growth in wisdom and love was a willingness to die, a self-giving; we see that the last revolution has in fact been prepared for by the revolutions that went before.

---

human society, it is of vital concern to the kingdom of God. For after we have obeyed the Lord, and in his Spirit nurtured on earth the values of human dignity, brotherhood and freedom, and indeed all the good fruits of our nature and enterprise, we will find them again, but freed of stain, burnished and transfigured. This will be so when Christ hands over to the Father a kingdom eternal and universal: "a kingdom of truth and life, of holiness and grace, of justice, love and peace". On this earth that kingdom is already present in mystery. When the Lord returns, it will be brought into full flower.' *Gaudium et Spes* 39.

It will, I suppose, be clear from what I have said that the relevance of christianity to human behaviour is primarily a matter of politics, it is concerned first of all with the media of communication, the structures of relationship within which men live. We are today emerging from an era in which christianity has been thought to be primarily about 'individual salvation', an era in which the gospel was held to be to do with the soul, a private and interior world, and to have only an accidental concern with the body and the public political world. Very few christians of our time would subscribe explicitly to this view but it has left behind a number of attitudes and assumptions that affect us often without our noticing. One of these is the assumption that christianity is first concerned with making people individually good, self-controlled, loving in their immediate personal relationships, chaste and so on. It is thought that if we have a lot of people like that around the place then larger political problems will be easier to solve. The business of christianity is to produce men of good will and then these men will produce a good society, or if they do not it does not matter very much because the people who are good in spite of a bad society will still be rewarded in heaven. (Those christians who have stopped believing in life after death think that good people are rewarded by some kind of peace of mind even in the midst of a flagrantly unjust society.)

Now the first objection to this is that a good man is hard to find in an unjust society. What we mean by a bad society is one in which men are hindered from loving and seduced into attitudes of domination and violence. The second objection is that men whose good will has been cultivated exclusively in immediate personal relationships amongst their families, friends, and acquaintances are quite frequently blind to large and devastating social injustice and to the agony of people whom they do not meet socially. It is quite common for people who advocate monstrous political behaviour to be described as 'personally' good men, kind to their children, tolerant and humble. I have in mind several politicians of the American right and a large number of people in South Africa. Christian belief, it is true, cannot be adequately stated in today's political terms, for no revolutionary belief can be stated in the terms of the society it subverts and christianity preaches the ultimate revolution; but the impact of christian belief is on the politics of the present.

There is a depressing tendency on the part of

both conservative and liberal christians to assume that discussions of christian morality are going to be mostly about sex. Sex is obviously a profoundly important mode of human communication, but to treat of it in isolation from all the other social, political and economic relationships between people is asking for trouble—asking for intellectual trouble I mean; in the practical field it is asking for a quiet life. So long as christian morality is thought to be mainly about whether and when people should go to bed, no bishops are going to be crucified. And this, as I say, is depressing. If the christian moralist is doing his job properly he has been promised that he will encounter the hostility of the world, of the established power structure.

To speak with vast and misleading generality, there is in the world at the moment a conflict between the dispossessed and the rich. The thesis of the rich (roughly speaking the western powers but for many purposes including Soviet Russia) is that the conflict is unnecessary, that if they were only left in peace they would be able to spread the benefits of the western way of life throughout the world. The thesis of the other side is that in the first place this does not in fact happen, the gap in living standards between poor and rich gets wider all the time,[1] and secondly that even if it were to happen it would not be desirable. The western way of life seems to these people a dominative society which left to itself produces not peace but repression and violence. The thesis of the dispossessed is not that they want simply a share in the capitalist world but that they want to create a new kind of community; they are, in fact, revolutionary. Whether the revolution towards which they are moving will be violent depends on the forms of repression adopted by the west.[2] Now there are, of course, no such simple monoliths as the 'dispossessed' and the 'west', and the struggle takes different and sometimes paradoxical forms in different parts of the world. Nevertheless we can say that there is 'a revolution' going on through-

[1] In order to spell out in some detail this broad statement I have included as an appendix to this book extracts from the Haslemere Declaration on aid to 'developing' countries.

[2] 'The revolution can only be peaceful when those who control the structures, the rich oligarchy, are willing to allow such a change to occur, recognising the long denied rights of the poor masses. To the degree that they oppose such a change, the masses will be forced to use ever more drastic measures, to take the power into their own hands and thus effect the change by themselves. It is the rich, then, with those of allied interests, who have the real say as to whether the process will be peaceful or violent. "Those who make pacific revolution impossible, make violent revolution

out the world today with at least as much truth as we could say that there was a 'revolution' going on throughout the different states of Europe in the nineteenth century. It took very different forms in Italy and Ireland and France but it would be pedantic not to see these separate events as interrelated and forming part of a single broad movement.

It seems to me that the first thing a christian will want to say about his moral position is that he belongs with this revolution. I say 'belongs with it' rather than 'belongs to it' because the christian revolution goes in and through this kind of revolution to something deeper, to the ultimate alienation of man which is sin and the ultimate transformation which is death and

---

inevitable" (J. F. Kennedy)' Fr Thomas R. Melville, 'Revolution is Guatemala's only Solution', *National Catholic Reporter* (Jan 31 1968), 5. cf 'One great source of the strength of the ruling class has ever been their willingness to kill in defence of their power and privileges. Let their power be once attacked either by foreign foes, or domestic revolutionists, and at once we see the rulers prepared to kill, and kill, and kill. The readiness of the ruling class to order killing, the small value the ruling class has ever set upon human life, is in marked contrast to the reluctance of all revolutionists to shed blood.' James Connolly, 'Conscription', in *The Best of Connolly*, ed Proinsias MacAonghusa and Liam Ó Réagáin, Cork 1967, 183.

resurrection. The revolution proclaims the historical mission and power of the dispossessed radically to change the structures of society. The outcast of society, precisely because he is outcast and has no stake within the community, because his class does not define itself in opposition to this or that other class within society but to the whole set-up, transcends the social order and thus his liberation liberates the whole community:

> There is a class in civil society which is not a class of civil society, a class which is the dissolution of all classes, a sphere of society which has a universal character because its sufferings are universal and which does not claim a particular redress because the wrong which is done to it is not a particular wrong but wrong in general . . . which claims no traditional status but only a human status . . . a sphere, finally, which cannot emancipate itself without emancipating itself from all the other spheres of society, without therefore emancipating all these other spheres.[1]

[1] Karl Marx, quoted by T. B. Bottomore and M. Rubel in *Karl Marx: Selected Writings in Sociology*, London 1963, 42.

The similarity between this view and the Old Testament teaching that the salvation of the unjust society will come about through the *anawim*, the dispossessed, is clear enough. But the New Testament goes further; for Jesus the 'poor' who possess the kingdom are, of course, in the first place the dispossessed, but he demands more of them than this: they must also be 'poor in spirit'; the community whose mission it is to transform the world is the community of *faith* which implies a dispossession of oneself which goes beyond even poverty and means, in the end, an acceptance of death. This means that the christian's relation to the revolution can never be a simple one, he needs to be constantly critical of the political revolution lest it should become a substitute for the final transformation of the world.

There is, as we have seen, a fundamental disagreement between christian and marxist concerning God; and this, as I have suggested, is a disagreement about the nature of revolution. However much the christian may do in the way of removing misconceptions about his theism (it is not an idolatry, etc) I do not see how this disagreement can ever be resolved at all except by the marxist abandoning his atheism or the christian his belief in the Father. This does not mean that they cannot work together at a certain level, as they plainly do in South America, Vietnam and elsewhere.[1]

As I see it, the christian commitment to the political revolution bears somewhat the same relation to his commitment to the final revolution, the resurrection, as does his belief in liturgical reform to his belief in the sacraments. I mean that the whole purpose of the liturgical reforms of Vatican II was to remove impediments to seeing the eucharist for what it is (and always has been). However successful we may have been in concealing from the people of God the true nature of the eucharist, the sacrament nevertheless remained itself. It is word of God which cannot be wholly silenced by words of men. In a somewhat similar way in those parts of the world (very few but of vast significance for the

[1] Guatemala's vice president Clemente Marroquin Rojas, writing in the daily *Impacto* of Guatemala City, charged that some church institutions there were 'fostering communist activities'. The church controls about 184 of the country's 5,600 educational institutions. 'This is not a matter of one nun or one priest or two priests' he said; 'there are many more like these among the abundant clergy. The government should conduct a detailed investigation of all residence permits to make sure there is no further danger that a whole generation of youths is converted to Marxism with the added fanaticism characteristic of the church.' 'Missioners back Guerrillas', in *National Catholic Reporter* (Jan 31 1968).

future) where at least parts of the church are plainly seen to be revolutionary[1] the church is appearing for what she really is (and always has been). Participation in the revolutionary movement of liberation is the social visibility of the life of faith. It would be absurd to deny that in general throughout the world the church is adept at concealing her true mission, but, to return to our analogy, she was for several centuries no less adept at concealing the true character of her sacramental life. (Consider, for example, how very rarely catholics received communion until this present century.)

The christian, then, cannot *identify* his christianity with participation in the revolution though he can certainly point to the absurdity of a christian not participating. The situation is finally much further clouded by the fact that both christians and other revolutionaries tend to betray their own revolutionary purpose. Christians tend to identify themselves with the establishment and so to regard any attack on this as an

[1] 'It is a simple fact that the church's teaching is now the most radical body of thought in Brazil, and that certain Catholic leaders, among the hierarchy and the laity, are the most revolutionary figures in Brazilian society.' Thomas C. Bruneau, 'The Church moves Left', *Commonweal* (Feb 2 1968). See also Appendix 2.

attack on the church. Marxists too tend to produce a fossilised bureaucratic society and to see the church as a focus of organised opposition to their domination. Amidst all these complications it is not surprising, nor even undesirable, that the relations between christians and other revolutionaries should remain slightly uneasy.

It has always been the fate of the christian church to be surrounded by alternatives that look more attractive at the time but which belong too much to their time and which later on we see to have been by-ways departing from the main road. Our own time is no exception. If the revolution is what is needed it seems absurd to suggest that it is to be found more truly in the church than in, say, the communist party. And yet even this proposition no longer looks so absurd as it did. Already the orthodox communist parties of many South American countries are accused of losing their revolutionary spirit. The christian will maintain that however attractive other movements may appear at the moment, and however important it may be to support them, in the end, because they settle for less than the final revolution, they will be found to betray their own purpose and fulfil a reactionary role. Christianity is, in a sense slightly different from Debray's, 'the revolution in the revolution' constantly recalling the revolutionary to his own purpose. Christianity alone, because it is the articulate presence of Christ, the future of mankind, cannot (however hard it sometimes seems to try) wholly betray its mission. As it seems to me, like St Peter and the twelve, we remain christians because there is nowhere else to go: if christianity is not the revolution, nothing else is.

I have not, in this book, tried to apply christian principles to particular moral questions because it seems to me that christianity does not in the first place propose a set of moral principles. As I suggested in my first chapter, I do not think that such principles are out of place in christianity; without them the notion of love may collapse into vagueness and unmeaning, but christianity is essentially about our communication with each other in Christ, our participation in the world of the future.

We have not a code of conduct—except in the crudest sense in which we may dismiss certain kinds of behaviour as obviously incompatible with the kingdom—we propose a way of life, a way of discovering about the depths of life, out of which decisions about our behaviour will emerge. The way to make an accurate christian assessment of a moral problem is to have been for some time immersed in the christian task of overcoming the world.

St Paul's moral teaching is placed in this perspective, the perspective of hope. He does not speak as though legislating for an achieved static society but as deciding what is best to do during the conduct of a revolutionary struggle. The whole moral discourse of Romans 12–15 is set in the context of christian hope and we may end with his opening words:

> Do not be conformed to this world but be transformed by your new mind. That is the only way to discover the will of God and know what is good, what it is that God wants, what is the perfect thing to do. [Rm 12:2]

# Appendix 1 The Haslemere Declaration

The Haslemere Declaration on world poverty was published on 26th March 1968 by a group of people concerned about 'the near-total failure by rich industrialised countries such as Britain to face the growing social and economic crisis in the "underdeveloped" two-thirds of the world. In January some of those concerned with overseas aid in Britain met to discuss what action could be taken. Most of this group work for organisations directly involved, such as the Catholic Institute for International Relations, Christian Aid, the Overseas Development Institute, Oxfam, Youth Against Hunger, etc, but this campaign is launched in their capacity as individuals.'

Part of the Declaration follows:

Most of the 'developing world' is *not* developing.

If the existing policies, complacency and lack of interest of the governments of the industrialised nations continue, it is unlikely they will ever help it to do so.

'Overseas aid' is largely a myth: at best a wholly inadequate payment for goods received, at worst another name for the continued exploitation of the poor countries by the rich. . . .

. . . The economic system that dominates the trading arrangements of the world today (even communist trade to a significant extent) may not be *consciously* exploitative but often, in practice, it subjects the needs of the poor to those of the rich. It has established a legacy of institutions, attitudes and rules of behaviour which makes it difficult to effect radical changes in the economic pattern. Thus the rules of the 'international economic game' are largely formulated by the rich: to suit their convenience, to resolve their problems. The game and its rules have evolved through the exercise of economic power; the rules are changed through bargaining from strength, through the 'swapping' of concessions. The economically and politically weak have little to offer and therefore get little in return. The poor countries cannot play this game. The Kennedy Round is a recent case study of these unpalatable facts: the poor were virtually ignored as the rich concentrated on making their own lives easier by horse-trading tariff reductions. Aid and the few concessions in trade that have been made to the poor have so far only *marginally* tempered the effect of this present system on the developing world.

To understand the nature of the relationship between the rich and the poor worlds we must just go back into history.

Europe began to dominate Africa, Asia, and Latin America during the seventeenth and eighteenth centuries. The economies of these countries were orientated often forcibly to the economic needs of the West—to produce the raw materials—oils, rubber, sisal, copper—that were needed for their growing industries, and sugar, cocoa, spices, ivory and gold for their growing populations.

## Truncated development

Indigenous patterns of development were truncated, traditional industries, such as textiles and metals, were driven out of existence by cheap imports from the low cost factories of the industrial slums of Europe—Lancashire in particular. Skills acquired over centuries began to disappear, making the day when the developing nations could make their comeback even more distant. More serious was the slave trade that decimated parts of the African continent: the Euro-American trade from the West and the Arab from the East. The whole structure of these advancing societies was torn apart, families split, towns pillaged, and many millions carted off, two-thirds to die on route and the rest to become the chattels of white plantation owners in the Americas.

Even where there were not the particular destructive effects of the slave trade, foreign intervention produced serious social consequences. Traditional patterns of authority were usurped, natural social boundaries ignored, patterns of land use arbitrarily changed and unstable urban agglomerations created overnight. Europe appeared to have little understanding and no respect for traditional religions. Civilisation was seen as synonymous with Europe's brand of Christianity: it was introduced often by irrelevant social and financial inducements.

The third consequence of Europe's economic and political domination was the introduction of a lone benefit—medical science—passed on in isolation from all other things that must go with it—better farming methods and industrialisation. As a result, over the last 200 years the level of living of Asia has probably *decreased*. The new spurt in population brought on by improved health facilities has pushed against a finite amount of land, whose productivity has remained almost static.

Fourthly, because of the West's long lead in economic development and its ubiquitous influence, the new industries and institutions that did grow in the developing countries were so structured that their survival and expansion depended on the European powers. Mines, factories, and estates imported their skills and machinery from Europe. The marketing of these products relied on access to the markets of the industrialised world. Their dependence on the rich countries for both exports and imports continues today. Production, and particularly know-how, is controlled by Western interests.

## Challenge to the West

Having built up over the last three centuries this firm, if unwitting, grip on the developing world, the West sees even the slightest swing of the pendulum away from its influence as a direct challenge—six Chinese engineers in Tanzania are seen as a 'threat', despite the presence of 2,000 Americans and British. The United States aid programme has until comparatively recently refused to be allied to any development project that took over functions which private enterprise could perform. Even as late as 1967 the US decided to withdraw its financial support for a large steel works in India, because it was to be publically owned.

The American aid programme operates in a way that makes new departures by developing countries who receive her aid extremely difficult.

Lest all this sounds like a too heavy indictment of the Western contribution, we hasten to add that we have a great respect for the valuable work done by those missionaries and administrators who gave their best in the developing world. It is unfortunate, however, they operated in a context and within a system that nullified much of their contribution.

**Economic domination**

In every attempt to escape from this spiral of economic domination, the poor world has been thwarted by the rich. They have tried to increase their exports to buy more of the things they needed from the industrialised countries. Exports have risen, sometimes sharply—but the prices for them have been steadily declining. For example:

(i) Two-thirds of Ghana's exports are cocoa. Between 1953 and 1961 cocoa exports increased by 71% in volume, but the revenue only increased by 23%. Meanwhile, European goods shipped to West Africa have gone up 25% in cost. This means that a machine that cost Ghana the equivalent of 10 tons of cocoa in 1953 costs 25 tons of cocoa in 1961.

(ii) Half of Brazil's exports are coffee. Between 1953 and 1961 coffee exports increased by 90% in volume, but the revenue fell by 35%.

(iii) Half of Malaya's exports are rubber. Between 1960 and 1961 rubber exports increased by 4% in volume, but the revenue fell by 35%.

Desperately trying to maintain their ability to import, the poor countries have borrowed money from the rich, accepted aid, and welcomed private investment. The result: still more economic dependence. They have to borrow more and more in order to repay past loans. Repayments already amount to the equivalent of two-thirds of the aid going to the developing countries, and by 1980 it is estimated that unless there is a pronounced increase in aid, the aid given will be entirely offset by repayments on past loans. Already Brazil has reached this unenviable position, and Argentina is sending back more to Britain than she receives from us. It is, as a former President of the World Bank has told us, as if we were 'doing nothing at all'.

The developing countries have tried to diversify exports. India and Pakistan, for example, produce low cost textiles. But when they showed that they were likely to capture most of the British textile market, on which British textile producers traditionally depended, Britain put quotas on the amount of their textiles that could be imported. The quotas only apply to 'low cost', that is poor countries, not to the exports of other rich countries.

### Subsidised industries

Developed countries even go to the lengths of subsidising domestic industries to keep them competitive in the face of cheap imports from developing countries. For example, Britain set up a highly-subsidised sugar-beet industry in East Anglia. The costs of its most efficient farmers are much higher than those of the most inefficient producers in the developing world. The Common Market countries are even planning to begin *exporting* their subsidised sugar production.

Commodity agreements have been introduced

to try and give developing countries a better deal but if the developing countries look like making a *major* breakthrough the rich call for the agreement to be re-negotiated. The latest example is coffee. Brazil, by setting up its own factories for processing coffee, has over the last few years captured 14% of the United States market in soluble coffee. America promptly threatened not to renew the International Coffee Agreement, which maintains stable prices, and talked about cutting aid to Brazil. The US soluble coffee manufacturers claimed 'unfair competition' because the Brazilian firms could buy coffee beans more cheaply than they could.

The reason: the Brazilian firms used broken coffee beans, unsaleable in the world market. But even without this 'unfair' advantage, they would inevitably be able to undercut US firms. Instant coffee weighs only one-third as much as beans, lowering shipping costs, and industrial wages in Brazil are lower than in the US.

But in March 1968 Brazil was forced to give way. The Brazilian Government has now undertaken to impose an export tax on Brazilian powdered coffee which will, in effect, make the broken beans sold by the Government as expensive to its own exporters of instant coffee as whole beans are to the American processors.

## Nationalisation

It is understandable, then, that developing countries consider taking the serious steps of refusing to repay their foreign debts and nationalising the foreign assets in their countries. This course grows increasingly attractive as more and more countries find they are spending more on repaying debts than they are earning. But it is easier said than done. The rich nations have a political strength that makes such initiatives almost impossible.

Chile, for example, a few years ago, needed to increase her exports. Her US-owned copper industry harboured a great potential, but the US companies were unwilling to increase production. Nationalisation of the copper industry would have been a solution, but the barriers appeared insuperable. The US would probably have cut off its large aid programme. There would probably then have followed a Cuban-style revolution with subsequent US military intervention. Finally the Chilean Government supplied the additional capital to enable the US companies to increase their production.

Guatemala, in 1953, faced a similar situation. The government decided to introduce land reform. It nationalised 400,000 acres of *uncultivated* land owned by the United Fruit Company of the USA, the largest landowner in the country. Compensation of $600,000 was offered—the amount at which the company had valued the land in its tax return. The offer was refused by the company. Backed by the US government, they demanded $16 million—almost five dollars for every man, woman, and child in Guatemala. This claim was rejected. There then followed a *coup d'état*. A military junta was established in power. One of its first acts was to return the land to the United Fruit Company.

Cuba's quarrels with the United States started less from ideology than from economics. Castro accepted a Russian offer to supply crude oil more cheaply than the US. The American companies in Cuba refused to refine it and were nationalised. The US promptly cancelled Cuba's sugar quota. At the end of this tit-for-tat came the Bay of Pigs and a total US trade embargo on Cuba.

## Tanzania's success

One country that has nationalised and survived is Tanzania. But it could only do so (*a*) because foreign investment and aid was small, (*b*) because the rich countries had already used their economic weapons (West Germany stopped aid because Tanzania wouldn't expel the East German consul from Zanzibar; Britain cancelled a £7 million loan because Tanzania broke off relations over Rhodesia); and (*c*) it is developing a philosophy that is determined to put self-respect and self-reliance before all else, despite the cost in aid reduction.

**Inadequate Aid**

Aid does little to repair this sad state of affairs. The developing countries of the world are left to finance 80% of their investment themselves. India, for example, requires for her Five-Year Plan an investment of £1,250 million a year. She receives 25% of it from outside. India's own people, who exist on an average of 1*s* 3*d* a day, put up the remaining 75%.

Britain spends more on defence than does the whole rich world on aid. America's defence budget is 60% greater than India's entire national income, although India's population is 2½ times that of the US.

If the US gave to every man, woman, and child in South Vietnam the money it is spending on the war each year, it is estimated that they would receive an income of £600 each, which would make South Vietnam the sixth richest nation in the world.

What is more, aid to the poor part of the world from the rich part of the world has gone down every year for the last seven years. In terms of the percentages of national incomes given, it has dropped by more than 30%, and is still falling. The outlook is bleak. This year the American aid budget, although the largest in the world, is the smallest since America began giving aid. It is likely to be even smaller next year. Britain over the last 15 months has cut back the budget of its Ministry of Overseas Development proportionately more than that of other government spending departments.

**Aid with strings**

Sometimes an offer of aid carries conditions which make it not worth accepting. For example, Peru was recently offered a large American loan on three conditions:

(i) that she buy US supersonic jets instead of French ones;
(ii) that she allow US ships to fish in Peru's territorial waters;
(iii) that she abandon attempts to gain a larger share of the US oil company's profits.

Peru rejected the loan.

Britain is not so clearly involved in strategic and private enterprise endeavours as the USA.

Unlike America, she does not have to find reasons to convince hostile congressmen why she should have an aid programme. It was a natural evolution as Empire gave way to Commonwealth.

This is not to say that Britain does not have a finger in the objectives of private enterprise and political strategy. For example, when the Indonesian confrontation came to an end two years ago and Sukarno lost his power, the UK offered £1 million to Indonesia, at a time when she was arguing her inability to extend more aid to Malaysia. And then as we have already noted there was the cruel withdrawal, in 1966, of a £7 million loan to Tanzania because of her radical criticism of British policy on Rhodesia.

France, another important aid-giving country, has also used her aid ruthlessly as a political weapon. When in 1958 Guinea chose independence rather than associate status with France, within forty-eight hours she withdrew her assistance programme, taking with her everything that was moveable including records, statistics, and even the telephones.

The communist countries, too, have equated the needs of the developing countries with their own national interests. The flow of vital exports to Cuba have been reduced in the last twelve months in an attempt to win Cuban support for Russian interests in the international Communist movement.

## Threatened interests

Aid, we repeat, varies from the sop of inadequate compensation to outright exploitation. The fact is that the rich countries have power and money and use both in their own interests. When poor countries threaten the interests of a rich country by effective competition a system of tariffs, quotas, or price-fixing is adopted to stop them. When real efforts are made to improve the international trading and monetary system (such as the Kennedy Round, or the creation of more liquidity), the interests of poor countries are largely ignored. In the horse-trading and bargaining of economic negotiations, the poor countries get nothing because they have nothing to bargain with. The Kennedy Round tariff cuts mainly affected products of interest to rich countries. When the rich forecast a possible shortage of international liquidity and agreed to create new liquidity—in the form of Special Drawing Rights in the IMF—they allocated most of it to themselves, with the rationalisation that poor countries would use it 'irresponsibly'.

When machinery is set up to conduct international negotiations with the avowed purpose of changing the economic system to favour the poor countries—as at UNCTAD—nothing happens.

### The UNCTAD conference

The poor countries can and do use their weight of numbers to pass resolutions, but the rich countries don't implement them. There have been absolutely no practical results from the first UNCTAD conference in 1964. At the second UNCTAD conference the rich countries have discussed tariff preferences for the manufactured exports of poor countries, and they have agreed to them in principle. But they show no signs of implementing them, and it is unlikely that they ever will.

The agreement over coffee prices has been renewed with Brazil cowed into absorbing effective competition. But no new commodity agreement has been established, and the discussions to start a cocoa agreement are in difficulties.

At the current UNCTAD meeting, the US and the UK have both pleaded they can't afford to spend 1% of their national income on aid. Germany, despite a large balance of payments surplus, says the same. So the poor countries have modified their request. They have asked the rich countries to spend 0·75% of their national income on aid. The chances that this request will be approved are small: the chances that, if approved, it will be met are smaller still. It would, in any case, be ineffective.

What should rich countries such as Britain do to break the spiral of economic exploitation and increasing dependency that marks the relationship between rich and poor?

## The Haslemere programme

The following is the outline of the programme we intend to campaign for. We believe that rich countries should:

1. Refrain from using their economic and political power to thwart the efforts of poor countries to gain a larger share of the benefits of trade and technology.
2. Refrain from economic retaliation and military intervention against poor countries which take political initiatives of which they disapprove.
3. Abolish all quotas and other special protective devices applied by developed countries to the manufactured exports of poor countries. No new ones should be introduced. Compensation for interests in rich countries damaged by the loss of such protection should be made by the government of the rich country concerned.

4 Abolish all subsidies to agricultural production in rich countries competing with production in poor countries (with the possible exception of some temperate products such as wheat). Compensation again should, if necessary, be made by the government of the rich country concerned.

5 Raise the income received from primary commodities sold to us by poor countries in the same way that rich countries subsidise their own agriculture. It should be acknowledged that the bargaining position of agricultural producers tends to be weak and that the prices of their produce are particularly susceptible to fluctuation and long-term decline. International agreements to stabilise the prices of the poor countries' main commodity exports should be concluded soon—especially for cocoa, sugar, bananas.

6 Allow the poor countries to erect trade barriers against the rich if they so wish.

7 Change the conventions governing international trading relations so that poor countries are helped, not discriminated against.

8 Cancel all debts owed to them by the poor countries.

9 Commit themselves to greatly increased long-term and *automatic* transfer of resources to poor countries. The poor will then be in a position to pursue their own economic and social policies. This will avoid the present situation in which aid has unacceptable political and economic strings. More specifically, we suggest the following lines of action:

(*a*) all transfer of financial resources from rich countries to poor should go through an international institution. We believe that the IMF is the most suitable. There should be a universal formula decided in advance, on how this automatic transfer of aid should take place. We suggest that the criteria of size of population and degree of poverty are the ones that should determine how much each country should receive. The rich countries for their part would give in proportion to their wealth. The transfer of aid should be committed for periods of at least five years ahead at a time. Unlike most aid given today it should be in the form of grants not loans. The developing countries have, given time to adjust, an unlimited capacity to absorb such aid. But as an approximate goal we suggest that rich countries should provide £3,000 million by 1970, £6,000 million by 1975, and £20,000 million by 1980. This compares with the £2,280 million the rich are giving at present;

(*b*) the impending reforms in the international monetary system offer another channel of help to the developing countries. A new form of international liquidity besides gold and the reserve currencies of sterling and dollars is to be created. When this is allocated to the member countries of the IMF we suggest that it goes, not mainly to the rich nations as presently planned, but only to the poor. Rich countries would then have to *earn* the new international money created by exporting to poor countries, rather than having it allocated free.

10 Rich countries should collectively recognise that poor countries do not need to adopt our way of life and may in fact be threatened by it. They should welcome and sympathise with attempts to create societies different from their own. Tanzania is an example of what we mean. The Arusha

Declaration of February 1967, made by the governing party of Tanzania, charts a course of economic and social development that will attempt to build on traditional African society rather than trying to propel traditional society into an unknown world of massive urbanisation, industrialisation, and dependence on foreign investment and aid. Julius Nyerere, President of Tanzania, talks of it in these terms: 'the growth must come out of our roots, not through the grafting on to those roots of something which is alien to them. This is very important, for it means that we cannot adapt any political "holy book" and try to implement its rulings with or without revision. It means that our social change will be determined by our own needs as we see them, and in the direction that we feel to be appropriate for us at any particular time.'

Nyerere continues, 'inherent in the Arusha Declaration, therefore, is a rejection of the concept of national grandeur as distinct from the well-being of its citizens, and a rejection too of material wealth for its own sake. It is a commitment to the belief that there are more important things in life than the amassing of riches, and that if the pursuit of wealth clashes with things like human dignity and social equality then the latter will be given priority. . . . With our present level of economic activity, and our present poverty, this may seem to be an academic point; but in reality it is very fundamental. So it means that there are certain things which we shall refuse to do or to accept, whether as individuals or as a nation, even if the result of them would give a surge forward in our economic development.'

*(The full text of the Haslemere Declaration is obtainable from 515 Liverpool road, London N7.*

# Appendix 2 Gospel and revolution

## by sixteen bishops of the Third World[1]

1. As bishops of some of the peoples who are striving to develop, we endorse the anxious appeal of Pope Paul VI in his letter *Populorum Progressio*, so as to define their duties for our priests and faithful, and to send words of encouragement to all our brothers in the Third World.

[1] This document was originally published in *Témoignage Chrétien* on 31 August 1967. The translation here, by Mr James Gordon, was first published in *New Blackfriars* (December 1967).

The original signatories numbered 15, but one more bishop has since signified his wish to be associated with the document. They are therefore as follows: Helder Camara, Archbishop of Récife, Brazil; John-Baptiste Da Mota e Albuquerque, Archbishop of Victoria, Brazil; Luis Gonzaga Fernandes, Auxiliary of Victoria, Brazil; Georges Mercier, Bishop of Laghouat, Sahara, Algeria; Michel Darmancier, Bishop of Wallis and Fortuna, Oceania; Amand Hubert,

2. As they are in this Third World, our churches are caught up in a confrontation no longer simply of east and west, but of three great groups: the western powers which grew rich in the last century, the two communist countries that have also become great powers, and finally the Third World, still seeking an escape from the domination of the great powers, and the freedom to develop in its own way. Within even the developed countries there are still classes, races and peoples that have not yet received their rights to a full human life. An irresistible urge is pushing these poorer elements towards their betterment by liberating them from all oppressive forces. Although most countries may have gained their political freedom, economic freedom is still a rarity. Few also are countries where social equality prevails, an

---

Vicar Apostolic, Heliopolis, Egypt; Angelo Cuniberti, Vicar Apostolic of Florencia, Columbia; Severino Mariano de Aguiar, Bishop of Pesqueira, Brazil; Frank Francic, Bishop of Split, Jugoslavia; Francisco Austregesilio de Mesquita, Bishop of Afogados de Ingazeira, Brazil; Gregory Haddad, Melchite Auxiliary of Beirut, Lebanon; Manuel Pereira Da Costa, Bishop of Campina Grande, Brazil; Charles Van Melckebeke, Bishop of Ning Hsia (China), Apostolic Visitor to Singapore; Antonio Batista Fragoso, Bishop of Crateus, Brazil; Stephen Loosdregt, Bishop of Vientiane, Laos; Waldyr Calheiros de Novais, Bishop of Volta Redonda, Brazil.

essential condition of true brotherhood, for peace cannot exist without justice. The peoples of the Third World are the proletariat of existing humanity, exploited by the great, their very survival threatened by ones who, because they are stronger, arrogate to themselves the sole right to judge and police peoples less rich in material terms. In fact our peoples are no less wise or just than the great powers.

## I. Independence in the face of political, social and economic systems

3. Revolutions are and have been part of the evolution of the world. Nor is this surprising. All the constitutions in force today originated at a time more or less distant from a revolution, that is to say from a break with some system that no longer ensured the common good, and the establishment of a new order more likely to bring it about. All revolutions are not necessarily good. Some are only palace *coups d'état*, and result only in a change of oppressor. Some do more harm than good, 'engendering new injustices . . .' (*Populorum Progressio*). Atheism and collectivism, to which some social movements have thought it necessary to commit themselves, are serious dangers to humanity. Yet history shows that some revolutions have been

necessary, that they have abandoned their original opposition to religion, and have produced good fruits. There is no longer any dispute about the French Revolution of 1789, which made possible the declaration of human rights (cf *Pacem in Terris* 11–27). Several of our countries have had to bring about these radical reforms, and are still having to. What should the attitude of christians and churches be to this? Paul VI has already shown us the way in his encyclical on the progress of peoples (*Populorum Progressio* 30–32).

4. From the doctrinal point of view the church knows that the gospel demands that first fundamental revolution which is called 'conversion', a complete return from sin to grace, from selfishness to love, from pride to a humble willingness to serve. This conversion is not merely internal and spiritual; it affects the whole man, his physical and social as well as his spiritual and personal being. It has a communal aspect laden with implications for all society, not only for life on earth, but more for the eternal life in Christ who, himself raised from the earth, draws all humanity to him. Such in the eyes of a christian is the integral flowering of man. Besides, for twenty centuries, visibly or invisibly, within or outside the church, the gospel

has always been the most potent ferment of deep social change.

5. Nevertheless, throughout her historical pilgrimage on earth, the church is in practice always tied to the political, social and economic system that in a given period ensures the common good, or at least an ordered society. So much so that sometimes the churches may seem to be fused with such a system, united as if in wedlock. But the church has only one bridegroom and that is Christ. She is in no way wedded to any system, least of all to the 'international imperialism of money' (*Populorum Progressio*), any more than she once was to the monarchy and feudalism of the Ancien Régime, any more than she will be in the future to some form of socialism. A glance at history is enough to show that the church has survived the ruin of systems who thought they had to protect her interests, or that they could make use of her. Today the social doctrine of the church, reaffirmed at Vatican II, is already dissociating her from this imperialism of money, one of the forces to which she was for a time tied.

6. Since the council voices have been raised, forcefully demanding an end to this temporary collusion between the church and money which is condemned from so many sides. Some bishops

have already set the example.[1] We ourselves have a serious duty to examine our position on this question, and to free our churches of all trace of dependence on great international finance. 'You cannot serve both God and mammon.'

7. In face of the recent development of this imperialism of money, we must remind ourselves and the faithful of the warning given by the seer of Patmos to the christians in Rome, when its fall was imminent, a great prostituted city, living in a luxury earned by the oppression of peoples and slave traffic: 'Go out from her, my people; that you be not partakers of her sins, and that you receive not of her plagues' (Rev 18:4).

8. In what is permanent and essential, namely her faithfulness to and communion with Christ in the gospel, the church is never in the pay of political, economic or social systems. As soon as a system ceases to ensure the common good to the profit of some party involved, the church must not merely condemn such injustice, but dissociate herself from the system of privilege, ready to collaborate with another that is better adapted to the needs of the time, and more just.

[1] *Populorum Progressio* gives the example of the late Bishop of Talca (Chile), Manuel Larrain.

## II. Faithfulness to the people

9. All of this applies to christians as well as their leaders in the hierarchy and the churches. We have not here abiding cities—Christ our leader willed to suffer outside the town (Heb 13: 12, 14). Let none of us cling to our privileges and our riches, but let each stand prepared to 'share what he has, for such sacrifices are pleasing to God' (Heb 13:16). Even if we have not succeeded in acting with goodwill and love, let us at least be able to recognise the hand of God correcting us as a father might a son in situations where this sacrifice is forced upon us (Heb 12:5).

10. We do not judge or condemn any of those who believe conscientiously that they must go into exile to preserve the faith in themselves and their children. The only ones who should be strongly condemned are those who evict populations by material or spiritual oppression, or by the appropriation of their lands.

Christians and their pastors are dedicated to remaining among the people in their own country. History shows that it is seldom a good thing in the long run for a people to take refuge in exile far from their native land. It must either defend itself effectively against the alien aggressor, or else accept such reforms as are necessary.

It is a mistake for christians to cut themselves off from their country and people in the hour of trial, particularly if they are rich, and would only flee to preserve their affluence and their privileges. It is true that a family or an individual may have to emigrate to find work, in accordance with the right of emigration (cf *Pacem in Terris*). Yet a large-scale exodus of christians could lead to crisis. It is on their own soil and among their own people that christians are normally called to live, in solidarity with their brothers, of whatever religion, that they may be living witnesses among them to the love Christ has for all.

11. As for us priests and bishops, our duty to remain where we are is even more pressing; for we are the representatives of the good shepherd who, far from fleeing like a mercenary in the hour of danger, remains in the midst of his flock, ready to give up his life for his own (Jn 10:11–18). Jesus does tell the apostles to go from town to town (Mt 10:23), but this is strictly in a case of personal persecution for the faith; during a war or revolution involving the people with whom the pastor feels solidarity the case is quite different. If the people itself decided to go into exile, the pastor might follow his flock. But he cannot consider only his own safety, nor seek it in the company of a few profiteers or cowards.

12. Furthermore, christians and their pastors should know how to recognise the hand of the Almighty in those events that from time to time put down the mighty from their thrones and raise up the humble, send away the rich empty-handed, and fill the hungry with good things. Today 'the world persistently and urgently demands recognition of human dignity in all its fullness, and social equality for all classes'.[1] Christians and all men of good will cannot do otherwise than ally themselves with this movement, even if it means renouncing privilege and fortune for the good of the human community, in a greater conception of society. The church is by no means the protectress of great properties. She insists, with John XXIII, on the sharing of property, since property has primarily a social purpose.[2] Recently Paul VI recalled St John's words: 'But if any one has the world's goods and sees his brother in need, yet closes his heart against him, how does God's love abide in him?' (1 Jn 3:17), and those of St Ambrose: 'the earth is given to everyone, and not only to the rich' (*Populorum Progressio* 23).

13. All the fathers, of the east as well as of the west, repeat the words of the gospel: 'Share out

[1] Patriarch Maximus IV at the council, 27 October 1964.
[2] *Mater et Magistra*, 389–391.

your harvest with your brothers. Share ye our crops, which tomorrow will have rotted away. What shocking avarice for a man to leave all to mildew sooner than leave part of it to the needy! "Whom am I wronging", says the miser, "in keeping what belongs to me?" All right, but tell me, what are these goods that belong to you? Where have you got them from? You are like a person who, taking his place at the theatre, would like to stop others coming in, meaning to enjoy by himself the spectacle to which all have an equal right. This is what rich people are like: proclaiming themselves sole masters of common goods that they have monopolised, merely because they were the first to possess them. If each kept only what is required for his current needs, and left the surplus for the needy, wealth and poverty would be abolished. . . . The bread you keep belongs to another who is starving, the coat that lies stolen in your chest to the naked, the shoes that rot in your house to the man who goes unshod, the money you have laid aside to the poverty-stricken. In this way you are the oppressor of as many people as you could help. . . . No, it is not your rapaciousness that is here condemned, but your refusal to share' (St Basil, 6th homily against wealth).

14. Taking into account certain necessities for

certain material progress, the church has for a century tolerated capitalism with its legalisation of lending at interest and other practices that so little conform to the moral teaching of the prophets and the gospels. She cannot but rejoice to see another social system appearing that is less far from that teaching. It will be the task of tomorrow's christians to follow the initiative of Paul VI, and channel back to their true sources, which are christian, these currents of moral strength, solidarity and brotherhood (cf *Ecclesiam Suam*). Christians have the duty to demonstrate 'that true socialism is a full christian life that involves a just sharing of goods and fundamental equality'.[1] Far from sulking about it, let us be sure to embrace it gladly, as a form of social life better adapted to our times, more in keeping with the spirit of the gospel. In this way we shall stop people confusing God and religion with the oppressors of the poor and of the workers, which is what the feudal, capitalist, and imperialist systems are. These inhuman systems have engendered others which, intended to liberate the peoples, in fact oppress the individual if they fall into totalitarian collectivism and religious persecution. But God and the true religion have nothing in common with the

[1] Patriarch Maximus IV at the council, 28 September 1965.

various forms of the mammon of iniquity. On the contrary, they are always on the side of any who wish to promote a more equitable and fraternal society involving all God's sons in this human family.

15. The church greets with joy and pride a new mankind that respects not money concentrated in a few hands, but the workers, the labourers, and the peasants. The church is nothing without him who never ceases to endow her with the power to thrive and so act, Jesus of Nazareth, who for so many years chose to work with his hands in order to reveal the outstanding dignity of workmen. 'The worker is infinitely superior to any amount of money', as a bishop of the council reminded us.[1] Another bishop from a socialist country declared: 'If the workers do not achieve some measure of control of their industries, all constitutional reform will be useless. Even if the workers sometimes receive better wages under some economic system, these increases alone will not satisfy them. In fact they want to own rather than sell their labour. Today the workers are increasingly aware that work is a part of being human. But a human being cannot be bought and sold. Any trading of labour is a form of

[1] Mgr G. Hakim, Archbishop of Galilee, at the council, 10 November 1964.

slavery. . . . This is the direction in which human society is progressing, even in a system reputedly less concerned with individual dignity than we are, namely marxism' (F. Francic, Split, Jugoslavia, 4 October 1965).

16. This is to say that the church rejoices to see developing in humanity forms of social life where work finds its proper place of predominance. As arch-priest Borovoi noted at the Ecumenical Council of Churches, we have made the mistake of adapting ourselves to the pagan juridical principles inherited from ancient Rome, but alas, in this sphere the west has sinned no less than the east. 'Of all the christian cultures, the Byzantine has done most to sanction social ills. It adopted uncritically all the social heritage of the pagan world and consecrated it. The civil law of the pagan Roman Empire was preserved under a cloak of ecclesiastical tradition for many more than a thousand years at Constantinople and in medieval Europe, and in Russia in the centuries since the period (sixteenth century) when our country began to think of herself as the heir of Byzantium. Yet it is utterly opposed to the social traditions of primitive christianity and of the Greek fathers, to the missionary preaching of our saviour, and all the teaching of the Old Testament prophets

who never grow old.' (Ecumenical Council of Churches. 12 July 1966. Church and Society, Geneva.)

## III. Faithfulness to God's word

17. There is no political aim of any kind behind our words. Our only source is the word of him who spoke through his prophets and apostles. The bible, particularly the gospels, denounce any attack on man created in God's image as a sin against him. Atheists today unite with believers in fulfilling this requirement of respect for the human being, working together in a common service of mankind in its search for justice and peace. Thus we can confidently address these words of encouragement to all men, for we all need courage and strength if we are to perform successfully the huge and urgent task of saving the Third World from poverty and hunger, and of freeing mankind from the catastrophe of a nuclear war: 'Never again war, away with weapons'.[1]

The poverty-stricken populations, in the midst of which the All-merciful has placed us as pastors of a small flock, know by experience that they can rely on themselves and their own efforts more than on help from the rich. Some rich

[1] Paul VI at the UN.

nations or some rich people among the nations do indeed offer a fair measure of help to our peoples, but we should be living in a delusion if we were to wait passively for a spontaneous conversion of all about whom our father Abraham warns us: 'neither will they be convinced if some one should rise from the dead' (Lk 16:31).

It is for the poor peoples and the poor among them to strive for their own advancement first of all. Let them regain confidence, let them educate themselves out of illiteracy, let them persevere in building their own destiny, let them develop, using all the methods that modern society puts at their disposal, schools, transistors, newspapers: let them hear the people who can waken and form the awareness of the masses, above all the words of their pastors, and let the latter give them in entirety the word of truth and the gospel of justice. Let the apostolic movements of militant laymen put into practice the exhortation of Pope Paul VI: '. . . It is for layfolk, by their free initiative, without waiting for orders and directives, to instil the christian spirit into the mind, the customs, the laws, and the constitutions of the community they live in. Changes are necessary, deep reforms are indispensable: they must work with determination to breathe into them the evangelical spirit . . .' (*Populorum Progressio* 81).

Finally, let the poor and those who are working for them unite, for union is the only strength of the poor, to insist on and promote justice in truth.

19. It is indeed truth and justice for which the people are above all hungry, and all who are responsible for instructing and educating them must busy themselves about it zealously. Some false conceptions must at once be removed: it is not true that God wishes there to be rich men enjoying the good things of this world by exploiting the poor: it is not true that God wishes there to be poor people always wretched. Religion is not the opium of the people. Religion is a force that exalts the humble and casts down the mighty from their seats, that gives bread to the hungry and reduces to hunger the over-eaters. Jesus certainly forewarned us that the poor would always be with us, but this is because there will always be the rich to amass the goods of this world, and also there will always be some inequalities due to varying capabilities and other unavoidable factors. But Jesus teaches us that the second commandment is equal to the first, for a man cannot love God without loving men his brothers. He warns us that all of us will be judged according to a single text: 'I was hungry, and you gave me to eat . . . it was I who was hungry' (Mt 25:31–46). All the great religions,

all mankind's systems of wisdom echo this text. The Koran declares the final test to which men are subject at the moment of God's judgement: 'What is this test? It is to buy back captives, to feed orphans at a time of famine . . . or the poor man sleeping on the hard ground . . . and to make for oneself a law of pity' (Sour 90:11–18).

20. It is our duty to share our bread and all our goods. If some claim the right to amass for themselves what is needed for others, then it becomes a duty for public authorities to enforce sharing which has not been done voluntarily. Pope Paul VI reminds us of it in his latest encyclical: 'The common good, then, sometimes calls for the expropriation of certain properties that on account of their size, their small development or complete lack of it, the poverty inflicted on the population, or the considerable damage done to their country's interests, constitute an obstacle to collective prosperity. Stating it clearly, the council reminded us no less forcibly that the available funds are not to be left to the careless whims of the individual, and that egotistical speculation must be banned. Consequently, citizens blessed with copious incomes arising from the national resources and effort cannot be allowed to transfer a large part of it abroad solely for their personal profit, careless of the manifest

wrong they are inflicting on their country' (*Populorum Progressio*). Nor can rich foreigners be allowed to come for the purpose of exploiting our poverty stricken peoples under the pretext of business or industry any more than a few rich people can be suffered to exploit their own peoples. This is what causes bitter nationalism, which is always to be deplored and which is the opposite of real collaboration between peoples.

21. What is true of individuals is also true of nations. Unfortunately, there is today no effectual world government able to enforce justice between peoples and to distribute goods justly. The economic system now in force permits rich nations to grow even richer, even when they are giving a little help to poor nations, which are growing proportionately poorer. The poor nations must therefore insist, using every legitimate means within their power, on establishing a world government in which all peoples without exception are represented and which can ask for, even enforce, a just sharing of goods, a state of affairs essential for peace. (cf *Pacem in Terris* 137; *Populorum Progressio* 78.)

22. Even within every nation, the workers have the right and duty of forming real trade unions to insist upon and to defend their rights: fair wages, paid holidays, social security, family

allowances, co-ownership . . . it is not enough for rights to be acknowledged on paper through laws. The laws must be implemented and governments must exercise their powers in this respect in the service of the workers and the poor. Governments must labour to bring to an end the class war which, contrary to what is usually maintained, has been unleashed, only too often, by the rich, who continue to wage it against the workers by exploiting them with inadequate wages and inhuman working conditions. Money has for a long time cynically waged a subversive war throughout the world, destroying entire peoples. It is high time that the poor peoples, upheld and guided by their lawful governments, should effectively defend their right to life. God did after all reveal himself to Moses, saying: 'I have seen the affliction of my people who are in Egypt, and have heard their cry because of their task masters . . . and I have come down to deliver them' (Ex 3:7–8). Jesus in fact took upon himself all mankind to lead it to eternal life, for which the earthly preparation is social justice, first form of brotherly love. When Christ frees mankind from death by his resurrection, he leads all human freedoms to their eternal fulfilment.

23. Thus we address to all men the gospel

words which some of us[1] addressed last year to their peoples who were subject to the same anxieties and spurred by the same hope as all the peoples of the Third World: 'We urge you to remain constant and dauntless, as evangelical leaven in the workers' world, relying on the words of Christ: "Look up and raise your heads, because your redemption is drawing near" (Lk 21:28).'

[1] Manifesto of bishops of the north-eastern region of Brazil. Récife, 14 July 1966.